Turkish
Cooking

Turkish
Cooking

Tess Mallos

PERIPLUS

First published in the United States in 2006 by Periplus Editions (HK) Ltd.,
with editorial offices at 364 Innovation Drive, North Clarendon, VT 05759 and
130 Joo Seng Road, #06-01/03 Singapore 368357

ISBN-13 978-0-7946-5023-0
ISBN-10 0-7946-5023-6
Printed in Singapore

DISTRIBUTED BY

North America and Latin America (English Language)
Tuttle Publishing
364 Innovation Drive, North Clarendon, VT 05759-9436
Tel: (802) 773-8930 Fax: (802) 773-6993
Email: info@tuttlepublishing.com
www.tuttlepublishing.com

Japan
Tuttle Publishing
Yaekari Building 3F, 5-4-12 Osaki,
Shinagawa-ku, Tokyo 141-0032
Tel: (03) 5437-0171 Fax: (03) 5437-0755
Email: tuttle-sales@gol.com

Asia Pacific
Berkeley Books (Pte) Ltd
130 Joo Seng Road #06-01/03 Singapore 368357
Tel: (65) 6280-1330 Fax: (65) 6280-6290
Email: inquiries@periplus.com.sg
www.periplus.com

Commissioned by Deborah Nixon
Text: Tess Mallos
Photographer/Stylist: Vicki Liley
Designer: Avril Makula
Cover Design: Bettina Hodgson
Editor: Susin Chow
Project Coordinator: Bettina Hodgson
Production: Sally Stokes and Eleanor Cant
Photography credits (in Australia): Afghan Interiors, Newtown; Peppergreen, Berrima; Orian Continental Foods, Willoughby; Sultans Sisters, Berrima; Nomadic Rug Traders, Pyrmont
Photography page 36: Andrew Elton
Photography page 49: Alan Benson
Photography page 108: Andrew Warn © Tess Mallos

Set in Univers 55 on QuarkXPress

contents

introduction

I have known the food of Greece from childhood, but when I first met my husband, I was introduced to Turkish cooking, and Turkish versions of the familiar Greek cooking. My mother-in-law was born in the Turkish town of Nevşehir in Anatolia, where there was a rather large Greek community. She came to Australia with her mother and sister in 1923.

Following the maxim that the road to a successful marriage was to cook as well as my mother-in-law, I added Turkish recipes to my repertoire, changed spicing and flavorings of the many Greek recipes I liked to prepare, and I learned to cook his favorite—baklava. On our first trip to Turkey in 1978, I extended my knowledge of Turkish cooking further.

What is appealing about the food of Turkey is its subtle, but sometimes assertive, spicing, and its emphasis on cereals, grains, pulses, vegetables, fruits, nuts, and yogurt—the marketing success story of the twentieth century that shows no sign of abating. The trend to healthy eating includes a preference for simple natural foods and most of the ingredients desired, including olive oil, are to be found in the Turkish kitchen.

Many ingredients you will already have or be familiar with; the others will be readily available at Middle Eastern, Greek and Turkish food stores and at specialized food stores such as those stocking natural foods. The ingredients section will assist you greatly as it gives the various names for particular ingredients, and which substitutes, if any, may be used for unusual or hard-to-come-by ingredients.

Today, modern appliances such as the food processor, electric mixer, blender and bread maker, cut down on effort and preparation time. However, my mother-in-law's favorite appliance was always the brass pestle and mortar her mother carried all the way to Australia from Turkey, and used specifically for pounding cumin seeds for Izmir Köftesi.

Tess Mallos

Pronunciation

Turkey changed from the Arabic script in the 1920s. Her written language now includes accents. This guide will assist you with pronunciation of recipe names.

A/a as in past
E/e as in egg
I/ı as the second vowel in valid
İ/i as in pit
Ö/ö as the vowel in err
O/o as in over
Ü/ü as in unit
U/u as in put
C/c as in jam
Ç/ç as "ch" in chair
Ş/ş as "sh" in ship
Ğ/ğ is a soft, slightly aspirate "g," always between vowels
The Turkish alphabet contains no Q, W or X.

Turkey

Istanbul stands majestically astride Europe and Asia, symbolic of the nature of Turkish cuisine. The bridges straddling the Bosphorus link two culinary heritages, though each has in itself evolved through centuries of history.

In the 1920s Ataturk determined to Westernize all that is Turkey, including her cuisine. I am so glad that he did not complete this part of his project, though fried pastries using a choux pastry base and dondurmas (water ices) certainly look as though he made some attempt.

A tour of the Topkapi Palace in Istanbul, once home of sultans, princes, their wives and concubines, gives a further insight into Turkish cooking. The names of the recipes emphasize the romantic, exotic era when Turkey's cuisine was being developed: Sultan's Delight

(Hünkâr Beğendi), Ladies' Navels (Kadın Göbeği), Ladies' Thighs (Kadın Budu), Lips of the beauty (Dilber Dudağı), Dainty Fingers (Hanım Parmağı), and Swooning Imam (Imam Bayıldı)—the latter certainly not because of any of the former, I assure you.

In Turkey the sea and its gifts plays a large part in the lifestyle and the food. One favorite dish, Skewered Swordfish (Kılıç Şiş), is a Turkish delicacy long remembered by visitors. The aroma of fish cooking over glowing charcoal or by other means permeates the air around the shores of the Bosphorus—Sardines in Grape Vine Leaves (Sardalya Sarması), Stuffed Mussels (Midye Dolması), Baked Fish (Balık Pilaki), and many more. A favorite sauce served with many seafoods is Tarator, a delectable combination of ground nuts, garlic, olive oil and vinegar. Though hazelnuts are generally used, almonds, pine nuts and walnuts are sometimes substituted.

Döner kebap

This famous Turkish specialty is found throughout Turkey and other countries of the region, though it is definitely Turkish in origin. As it is impractical for home preparation, a description will have to suffice.

Even-sized rounds of boneless lamb, taken from a whole carcass, are marinated for 24 hours in a mixture of olive oil, vinegar, onion, parsley, thyme, oregano or other combinations of herbs. A long, very heavy spit is loaded with the meat, layers interspersed with slices of fat from the tail of the lamb. The bottom of the spit is fitted with a disc to keep the meat in place and the top is finished with a whole green pepper and a tomato for color. The loaded spit is then placed before a vertical fire of charcoal or electrically heated elements. It is motor-driven so that the kebap revolves to cook evenly. As the lamb cooks on the outside, it is deftly sliced off into a special pan and served immediately in pide (flat bread) with salad. The doner kebap is now prepared in many Western cities with ethnic groups, since it is as popular in Lebanon, Syria, Greece and Iraq as it is in its native Turkey.

The flavor of Turkish food

Turkey's cuisine, colored by its history, is a mixture of Oriental and Byzantine influences, with the subtlety of Western cuisine softening the impact. Yogurt would have to be one of the most important elements, its use stretching back into pre-history. While mostly enjoyed in its simple form, with perhaps a dash of salt or a sprinkling of sugar, yogurt is also married into soups, becomes a sauce with little effort, and imparts a delicious flavor to cakes and desserts.

Perhaps the next pillar of Turkish cooking would be its pilavlar, or pilaf, renowned in world cuisine and worthy of their place. In researching, writing and testing the recipes, I became aware that no matter how they were formulated there would be some cooks who would agree and others who would strongly disagree with my methods. This is the beauty of Turkish cooking: a dish is a reflection of the cook, her love of food, and her dedication to its preparation for the pleasure of her family.

Herbs are subtly used in Turkish cooking, predominantly parsley, dill, mint, bay leaves and to a lesser extent thyme and oregano. In spicing, pepper, bahar (allspice), cinnamon and paprika are the most widely used. A favorite Turkish garnish for foods is paprika steeped in oil. Circassian Chicken (Çerkes

Tavugu) goes one step further: a dedicated cook will painstakingly extract the oil from walnuts to blend with paprika for the garnish. This, by the way, would be without doubt one of the most delicious chicken dishes I have ever tasted.

Turkey produces a wide variety of fruit and vegetables, all excellent in their season, but tomatoes in summer are a special joy. A good Turkish cook would prefer to use fresh tomatoes rather than tomato paste, but certainly uses the latter when tomatoes are out of season.

Olive oil, safflower oil and butter are favored for cooking, though peanut or corn (maize) oil can be used for general frying, particularly for pastries. Olive oil is essential for vegetable dishes, not only for its flavor, but because such dishes are often eaten cold.

Eating Turkish style

The early days of the Ottoman Empire saw Istanbul (then called Constantinople) as a cosmopolitan city of Turks, Greeks, Armenians, Bulgarians, Circassians, Venetians, Genoese, Jews, Serbs and Arabs. With such a beginning, it is any wonder that confusion exists as to what is Turkish and what is not?

The point is that Turkish cuisine, as with most cuisines, has been shaped by its history, but the people of the country through ensuing generations have marked it indelibly so that it is now a cuisine with its own national character.

Perhaps Istanbul today is the epitome of all that is Turkish. Her streets are thronged with food vendors selling şiş kebapı and köfte in pide, with crisp cucumbers, bell peppers and tomatoes or simit (crusty bread rings smothered with sesame seeds), and with the lemonade and vişne (sour cherry drink) vendors, their highly-polished, ornate brass and glass tanks strapped to their backs or slung across their bodies.

If a Turk wants refreshment, whether bought from an itinerant vendor or from a shop or store, the opportunity is everpresent.

The coffee house is a favorite meeting place, a predominantly male domain, with coffee drinking an extremely popular pastime. Coffee was introduced to

Turkey by the Arabs, and in turn Turkey introduced it to Europe. However, tea is far more popular in Turkey, served in a delicate tulip-shaped glass on a saucer with two lumps of sugar alongside.

The pastry shops are a delight to the eye and a threat to the waistline. Lokum (Turkish Delight) is made in huge quantities with an unbelievable assortment of flavors, varying from the typical pink-colored confection flavored with rose water to one so filled with chopped nuts and dried fruit that the lokum in it just serves to hold the sweet gelatinous mass together.

One feature of entertaining in a Turkish home is the serving of an assortment of mezes. These are placed en masse on a table and so served. It is called a "raki table." Of course raki, a potent aniseed-flavored spirit of Turkey, is always served at such a gathering. And though the occasion might appear at first to resemble a Western cocktail party, it could continue until the early hours of the morning, with an everchanging assortment of hot and cold mezes being served.

While the serving of Turkish meals differs from house to house and between the city and rural dweller, it is basically the same. Meals are served Western-style at a table, with all the dishes for the meal placed on the table at the same time; however, in some rural areas, a low round table is used with diners sitting on the floor. Meat or chicken is generally combined with vegetables for a güveç or pilaki (casserole or stew). If kebap or köfte are prepared, a separate vegetable accompaniment would be served. A salad, either an elaborate assortment or a simple combination of one or two ingredients, plus pickles and yogurt and the inevitable pilav, are always present. Cheese, bread and fresh fruit complete the meal. The beverage is usually ayran (yogurt drink), particularly in summer.

When a Turk wishes to entertain in a grand manner, the range of recipes is such that a banquet to delight any gourmet can be prepared. It is not unusual to find Turks entertaining in such a way, particularly those who have a high social status. Many of the traditional recipes, such as Wedding Meat (Düğün Eti) and Noah's Pudding (Aşure), show the Turk's love of celebration.

ingredients and equipment

Cooking methods and equipment

While the household might have a modern stove, cooking on a charcoal fire is still very much preferred in Turkey. The Western barbecue, of whatever type, will serve you most satisfactorily. For food preparation, the pestle and mortar is an essential item of kitchen equipment. Cooking pots and pans are either tin-lined copper or aluminum, with a variety of pottery dishes for oven cooking. Any suitable Western cooking utensil can be used for Turkish cooking, with the addition of a food processor or blender to replace the pestle and mortar, though using the latter does give the cook a great deal of satisfaction.

For making Turkish coffee a small, long-handled coffee pot, called a "cezve," is essential and these are readily available at Middle Eastern stores. A small saucepan really does not give the same results.

Ingredients for Turkish cooking

There are few, if any, ingredients used in Turkish cooking which are difficult to obtain. Cosmopolitan influences have been felt in most Western countries and such foods are commonplace. One vegetable, the eggplant (aubergine), which is so much a part of Turkish cooking, is now widely known; however, recipes using this vegetable detail the Turkish methods for its preparation. The preferred variety of eggplant is the long purple fruit, but as this is only available during the summer you will have to choose the smallest possible oval eggplants at other times to produce dishes such as Swooning Imam (Imam Bayıldı). The following text and the glossary give further details on foods for Turkish cooking.

BELL PEPPERS (CAPSICUMS)
Bot: *Capsicum annuum*
Turkish: tatlı biber
Also know as sweet peppers, capsicum and pimento, these peppers are green, ripening to a deep red with a change in flavor when ripe. The spice paprika is made from the ripe pepper.

BULGUR (BURGHUL)
Turkish: bulgur
Hulled wheat, steamed until partly cooked, dried then ground. Available in fine and coarse grades. It has a nut-like flavor.

CHICKPEAS (GARBANZO BEANS)
Bot: *Cicer arietinum*
Turkish: nohut
Used as a food since ancient times. They must be soaked before cooking and some recipes require the removal of the skins. Ready-skinned chickpeas are also available. Also roasted as a snack food.

CHILI
Bot: *Capsicum frutescens*
Turkish: acı biber
When handling chilies, keep fingers away from mouth and eyes. Dried chilies or ground chili pepper may be substituted. Before using dried chili, remove seeds and soak chili in hot water for 5 minutes. Use ground chili pepper cautiously, adding a small amount at a time and tasting until the desired heat is obtained.

CILANTRO (CORIANDER)
Bot: *Coriandrum sativum*
Turkish: kişniş
A member of the parsley family. Both the fresh leaves (cilantro) and seeds (coriander) are used. The flavor of the leaves is an acquired taste; the name derives from the Greek "koris", meaning bug, indicative of its aroma. It is also similar to the aroma of dried orange zest.

CINNAMON
Bot: *Cinnamomum zeylanicum*
Turkish: tarçin
A popular spice for both savory and sweet dishes; either the ground form or pieces of bark are used. Cinnamon sticks or quills are made of fine sheets of the inner layer of the cinnamon bark, dried and interleaved to form layered tubes. In recipes, a small piece of bark refers to a stick about 1½ in (4 cm) long, and a large piece is about 3 in (8 cm) long; however, there is no need to be exact in measuring.

CLOVES
Bot: *Syzygium aromaticum*
Turkish: karanfil
The dried flower bud of an evergreen tree native to tropical Asia. Used in both savory and sweet dishes. A clove is sometimes added to simmering chicken to remove unwanted flavors, perhaps necessary for free-range chickens or boiling fowls, but not for specially-raised birds. It is claimed that cloves sweeten the breath after eating garlic.

CORNSTARCH (CORNFLOUR)
Turkish: mısır unu
A white starch used for thickening milk puddings and essential for making Turkish Delight (Lokum). Not to be confused with yellow corn flour.

CUMIN
Bot: *Cuminum cyminum*
Turkish: kimyon
Cumin seeds, from a plant native to Egypt, have been widely used as a spice in Eastern Mediterranean cooking since ancient times.

DILL
Bot: *Anethum graveolens*
Turkish: dereotu
Native to the Mediterranean region, dill was much favored as a medicinal herb in ancient times. The feathery leaves are blue-green and give a distinctive, slightly aniseed flavor to meat, vegetable and rice dishes, and pickles. An excellent herb with globe artichokes. Fennel may be substituted.

EGGPLANT (AUBERGINE)
Bot: *Solanum melongena*
Turkish: patlıcan
Recipes give details of preparation in most instances. Stem is left on if baking or grilling as it provides a convenient handle. Slice, cube or slit as directed in recipe, and either sprinkle generously with salt, or place in well-salted, cold water. Let stand for 30 minutes so that bitter juices are removed. Drain and pat dry with a clean kitchen towel or paper towels. The long (Japanese) eggplants do not need salting.

FAVA (BROAD) BEANS
Bot: *Vicia faba*
Turkish: fava
Used fresh in Turkish cooking. When very young, the whole bean is used, topped, tailed and strings removed. Mature beans are shelled; if large, the skins are removed. Frozen fava beans are a good year-round standby and are easily skinned.

FLOUR
The plain flour used in these recipes is known in North America as all-purpose flour; wholemeal flour is known as whole-wheat flour. Unbleached all-purpose (plain) flour can be used in recipes if preferred, especially for bread.

GARLIC

Bot: *Allium sativum*

Turkish: sarmısak

Used from ancient times for the medicinal properties attributed to it, garlic is essential and should not be omitted from recipes using it. Remember that the flavor of garlic becomes more pronounced if browned, so avoid browning if a strong flavor is not desired. Raw garlic, finely chopped, is often mixed through boiled greens. Any recipe using raw garlic will leave you with an unpleasant breath. Chewing on a clove or drinking milk are favorite antidotes.

MINT

Bot: *Mentha spicata*

Turkish: nane

The mint most favored is spearmint in fresh or dried form. Used in meat and vegetable dishes, fragrant when fried in butter or ghee for a final touch to yogurt soups and salads, mint gives a distinct and appealing flavor. Fresh and dried mint is readily available.

NIGELLA

Bot: *Nigella sativa*

Turkish: nigella

Often called black cumin, though not related to cumin, nigella seeds are aromatic with a peppery flavor. Used to flavor sweet yeast breads and as a topping for pide.

NUTMEG

Bot: *Myristica fragrans*

Turkish: küçük

The hard inner kernel of the fruit of a tropical tree grown in the West Indies, Sri Lanka and South-East Asia.

OKRA (LADIES' FINGERS)

Bot: *Abelmoschus esculentus*

Turkish: bamya

Also called gumbo. Native to Africa, okra is an angular pod tapering to a point. Young okra are preferred. The vegetable has viscous properties. The preparation of the vegetable is so devised that these properties are lessened. If you like the glutinous texture, then do not use the vinegar treatment given, though a brief blanching will firm the vegetable. Okra is also available dried, canned and frozen.

PREPARING OKRA

Wash well, handling okra gently. Trim stem end without cutting pod. If desired trim around conical stem attached to pod, removing a thin layer. This is the correct way to prepare okra, but it is time-consuming and only serves to remove the fine brown ring just above the pod and the outer layer of the stem. Dry okra well in a kitchen towel, or spread out and leave until dry. Place in bowl and add ½ cup (4 fl oz/125 ml) distilled vinegar to each 1 lb (500 g) okra. Toss gently so that vinegar coats okra. Let stand for 30 minutes, drain and rinse well. Dry and use as directed in recipes. The vinegar treatment prevents okra from becoming slimy during cooking.

OLIVES

Bot: *Olea europaea*

Turkish: zeytin

The fresh fruit is bitter and must be treated to make it edible. Though recommended methods use a lye solution initially, home-cured olives are prepared in other ways. Ripe olives are dry-salted in wicker baskets and left for several days until the bitter juices have run out, then placed in wooden casks to mature, giving olives a wrinkled appearance. Another method for both ripe and green olives requires soaking in water for 3–7 days (the longer period for green olives) with water changed daily; they are then left in brine to mature. Slitting or cracking green fruit hastens curing. Oil is extracted by pressing, the first pressing yielding the finest oil which is greenish in color. The pulp is treated and subsequent pressings give oil of gradually lessening quality. Better quality oils keep longest.

ORANGE FLOWER WATER

Turkish: portakal çiçegi suyu

A fragrant liquid distilled from orange blossoms and used to flavor sweets and pastries. If a concentrated essence is all you can obtain, use in drops rather than the spoon measures given.

PARSLEY, FLAT-LEAF (ITALIAN)
Bot: *Petroselinum crispum* var. *neapolitanum*
Turkish: maydanoz
In all recipes fresh flat-leaf (Italian) parley is used.
Curly parsley may be used for garnish.

PASTOURMA
Turkish: pastirma
Pastourma is the most widely used term for this dried,
highly-spiced beef popular in Turkey. Fenugreek, garlic,
paprika, black pepper and chili are the main
ingredients used in the thick, spicy coating. Slice very
thinly and eat with bread, or fry in butter and serve
with fried eggs. It is available at Greek food stores.

ROSE WATER
Turkish: gül suyu
Distilled from fragrant rose petals, rose water is used
for both savory and sweet dishes. As the strength
varies according to the quality, when using a new
brand, add cautiously and taste to judge how much is
required. Price is usually indicative of quality, with the
more expensive brands being stronger. Rose water
essence is a concentrate; it should be used in drops
rather than the spoon measures given.

SAFFRON
Bot: *Crocus sativus*
Turkish: safran
It takes the stamens of almost a quarter million
blooms to produce 1 lb (500 g) of saffron, which
makes saffron expensive. Buy a reliable brand as there
are cheaper versions sold which are not true saffron.
Pound threads in a mortar and soak in liquid specified
in recipe to bring out the fragrance and color.

SALEP
Turkish: salep
A fawn-colored powder from the dried tubers of
various species of orchids (*Orchis*). It has a gelatinous
quality similar to cornflour (cornstarch) or arrowroot.
In Turkey it is made into a hot beverage with milk and
sugar: 1 teaspoon salep to 1 cup (8 fl oz/250 ml) cold
milk, stir then heat until boiling; serve with a dusting
of ground cinnamon. Street vendors sell it in winter. It
is also available at Middle Eastern markets.

SCALLIONS (SHALLOTS/SPRING ONIONS)
Bot: *Allium cepa*
Turkish: yeşil soğan
Also known as shallots, spring onions and green
onions, these are the long green shoots of an
immature onion. Unless otherwise specified in recipe,
use some of the tender green tops as well as the white
section.

SESAME SEEDS
Bot: *Sesamum indicum*
Turkish: susam
Pale cream seeds of a plant grown in tropical regions.
Sesame seeds are oily and highly nutritious. The seeds
are used on breads and cookies, for halva, and for
tahini.

SPINACH AND SWISS CHARD (SILVERBEET)
Turkish: ıspanak
Spinach (*Spinacia oleracea*) should not be confused
with Swiss chard (*Beta vulgaris*)—two vegetables are
not even related botanically. Spinach, also known as
English spinach, is widely used in the Middle East. As
spinach has a short season, from midwinter to late
spring, frozen leaf spinach may be substituted at other
times. Swiss chard can be used instead of spinach, but
in some recipes the result is not quite the same. It is
preferable to cook spinach or Swiss chard in a
stainless steel or enamel pan, as aluminium can cause
discoloration.

SUMAK
Turkish: sumak
Dried, crushed red berries with a pleasant, lemony
flavor. These come from particular species of sumak
tree and it is important to purchase sumak from
Middle Eastern markets as related species of tree can
be poisonous.

Eggplant fritters Patlıcan kızartması

Serves 6
Cooking time about 20 minutes

3 long eggplants (aubergines), each
    about 8 oz (250 g)
salt
1 quantity beer batter (page 75)
oil for shallow frying

For serving:
Yogurt Sauce (Yogurt Salçası) (page 18) or
    Tarator (page 18)

Remove stems from eggplants and wash well. Peel skin in ½-in (12-mm) strips lengthwise to get a striped effect. Cut into ¼-in (5-mm) slices and spread on a tray. Sprinkle liberally with salt and let stand for 30 minutes. Pat dry with paper towels.

Make beer batter following directions on page 75.

Dip each eggplant slice into batter and shallow-fry in hot oil until tender and golden-brown on both sides, about 3 minutes. Drain on paper towels.

Serve hot with Yogurt Sauce or Tarator as an appetizer, or as a side dish to main meals.

VARIATIONS

Carrot fritters
Havuç kızartması

Substitute 1½ lb (750 g) large carrots for eggplants. Scrape carrots and slice diagonally in ¼-in (5-mm) pieces. Cook in boiling, salted water until just tender, about 5 minutes. Drain and pat dry, before dipping in batter as in recipe above.

Zucchini fritters
Kabak kızartması

Substitute 1½ lb (750 g) medium-sized zucchini (courgettes) for eggplants. Trim and cut lengthwise or diagonally into ¼-in (5-mm) slices, depending on how they are to be served. Salt if desired, but this softens them and they are better if slightly firm when cooked. Dip in batter and cook as in recipe above.

Hazelnut sauce
Tarator

Makes 2 cups (16 fl oz/500 ml)

1 cup (5 oz/150 g) shelled hazelnuts
1 cup (2 oz/60 g) soft white breadcrumbs
3 cloves garlic, crushed
1 tablespoon water
1 cup (8 fl oz/250 ml) olive oil
½ cup (4 fl oz/125 ml) white vinegar
1 teaspoon salt

Blanch hazelnuts if desired. Place in a bowl, cover with boiling water, and let stand for 5 minutes. Drain and peel off skins. This is not necessary, but I find it improves the flavor and appearance of the sauce.

Grind hazelnuts in a blender, food processor or nut grinder, or pound using a pestle in a mortar. If using grinder or mortar, transfer hazelnuts to a bowl when pulverized.

Add breadcrumbs, garlic and water, and process or beat by hand while adding oil in a thin stream. Gradually add vinegar, and beat well until smooth. Stir in salt. (The blender gives the smoothest sauce; other methods give a textured sauce.)

Transfer to a serving bowl and refrigerate to chill. Serve with seafoods, fried vegetables and plain cooked vegetable salads, or according to recipe directions.

NOTE: Though the true Turkish tarator is almost always prepared with hazelnuts, walnuts are sometimes used. Blanched almonds or pine nuts are also used, in which case add lemon juice instead of vinegar.

VARIATION: For Almond Sauce (Tarator), see page 68.

Yogurt sauce
Yogurt salçası

1–2 cloves garlic
½ teaspoon salt
1 cup (8 fl oz/250 ml) Yogurt (page 125)

Using a pestle, pound garlic with salt in a mortar. Alternatively use a garlic press and blend with salt.

Combine with yogurt, cover and refrigerate until required. Serve with fried vegetables, kebabs, and as specified in recipes.

Shortcrust pastry
Hamur

2½ cups (12½ oz/390 g) all-purpose (plain) flour
½ teaspoon salt
½ cup (4 oz/125 g) firm butter
1 egg yolk
⅓ cup (3 fl oz/90 ml) cold water

Sift flour and salt into mixing bowl. Cut butter into small pieces and, using fingertips, rub into flour until mixture resembles fine breadcrumbs.

Beat egg yolk lightly, and add to flour mixture with water. Mix to a soft dough then knead lightly until smooth. Cover and let rest for 20–30 minutes before using as directed in recipe.

Turkish bread Pide

Makes 3 breads
Cooking time 8–10 minutes

2½ teaspoons (¼-oz/7-g sachet) active dry
  yeast
½ teaspoon sugar
1½ cups (375 ml/12 fl oz) lukewarm water
4 cups (20 oz/600 g) strong bread flour or
  all-purpose (plain) flour
1 teaspoon salt
4 tablespoons olive oil
1 tablespoon toasted sesame seeds or nigella
  (black cumin seeds)

Dissolve yeast and sugar in ½ cup (4 fl oz/
125 ml) water. Sift flour and salt into a
mixing bowl, and make a well in center.
Pour in yeast mixture and remaining water.
Stir a little of flour mixture into yeast
mixture, cover and let stand for 10 minutes
in a warm place until frothy.

Pour oil into center. Mix to a soft
dough, adding a little extra water if dough
is too firm. Turn out onto a lightly floured
work surface and knead until smooth and
elastic, about 10 minutes. Only add extra
flour if dough remains sticky after a few
minutes of kneading. Shape into a ball,
invert a bowl over dough, and let rise until
dough has doubled in size.

Punch down dough and divide into
3 portions. On lightly floured work surface,
shape each into an oval about 8 in (20 cm)
long. Leave on work surface and, holding
thumb and two fingers together, make
4 deep depressions along center of bread
and along each side ½ in (12 mm) in from
edge. Cover with a kitchen towel and let
stand for 15–20 minutes. While loaves are
rising, preheat oven to 450°F (230°C/Gas 8)
with a large baking sheet placed on center
shelf of oven.

Brush loaves lightly with water and
sprinkle with sesame seeds or nigella. Pick
up one loaf by sliding hands underneath,
then lift and gently pull out to stretch to
about 10–12 in (25–30 cm) long. Drop onto
hot baking sheet in oven, leaving room for
other loaves, and close oven door
immediately to retain heat. Repeat with
remaining loaves. Bake until lightly
browned and loaves sound hollow when
tapped, 8–10 minutes. Cool on a wire rack
and use on day of baking or wrap well and
freeze. Serve with dips and main meals.

NOTE: If your baking sheet is of normal
size, bake one loaf at a time, removing
bread and returning baking sheet to oven
to reheat before cooking the next loaf.

Baked filo rolls Burma böreği

Turkey is famous for its börekler—delicate pastries filled and shaped in various ways. The role of börekler in Turkish cuisine is not merely as an appetizer or first course: they are often served as an accompaniment to light soups, and the more substantial versions are served as main dishes.

While a simple homemade hamur (shortcrust pastry, page 18) is usually used, yufka (filo pastry) is also popular. For the cheese filling, a homemade, cottage-style cheese called beyaz peynir is usually used. It is very similar to ricotta in flavor; however, when salted, it is somewhat akin to feta. Use either of the fillings given in this recipe, or double the amount of filo pastry and butter and make both fillings.

Makes 30
Cooking time about 45 minutes

10 sheets Yufka (Filo Pastry) (pages 28–9)
½ cup (4 fl oz/125 ml) melted unsalted butter

For cheese filling:
1¼ cups (6 oz/185 g) beyaz peynir (feta cheese)
¾ cup (6 oz/185 g) ricotta or cottage cheese
4 tablespoons finely chopped fresh flat-leaf (Italian) parsley
1 egg, beaten
freshly ground black pepper

For meat filling:
2 tablespoons butter
2 tablespoons pine nuts
1 large onion, finely chopped
1 lb (500 g) ground (minced) lamb or beef
2 tablespoons chopped fresh flat-leaf (Italian) parsley
½ teaspoon ground cinnamon
salt and freshly ground black pepper

Leave filo pastry in its package at room temperature for 2 hours before unfolding. Stack sheets of filo and cut stack crosswise evenly into thirds, using ruler and craft knife. Width of pastry becomes length of strips; strips should be approximately 6 in (15 cm) wide and 11–12 in (28–30 cm) long. Stack strips and cover with folded clean dry kitchen towel topped with a moistened towel.

To make cheese filling: Mash cheeses together in bowl and stir in parsley, egg and pepper to taste.

To make meat filling: Melt butter in frying pan, add pine nuts and cook until golden, about 2–3 minutes. Using a slotted spoon, transfer to a plate. Add onion to pan and cook gently until soft, about 10 minutes. Increase heat, add meat and cook until juices evaporate and meat begins to brown, about 10 minutes, stirring often to break up lumps. Add pine nuts, parsley, cinnamon, and salt and pepper to taste. Let cool.

To make börekler: Take 2 filo strips at a time, brush 1 strip with melted clarified butter and top with other strip. Butter top of strip, and with narrow end toward you, place about 1 tablespoon chosen filling along end, ¾ in (2 cm) in from base and sides. Fold filo over filling, fold in sides and brush side folds with butter. Roll up in cigar shape and place seam-side down on a greased baking sheet. Brush top with butter. Repeat with remaining filo strips and filling.

Bake in a preheated oven at 350–375°F (180–190°C/Gas 4–5) until golden, about 20 minutes. Serve hot.

Stuffed grape vine leaves
Yalancı asma yaprağı sarması

Makes 6 dozen
Cooking time: 1¼ hours

For rice filling:
½ **cup (4 fl oz/125 ml) olive oil**
2 **large onions, finely chopped**
1 **cup (7 oz/220 g) short-grain rice**
¼ **cup (1½ oz/45 g) pine nuts**
¼ **cup (1½ oz/45 g) currants**
1 **teaspoon ground allspice**
2 **tablespoons finely chopped fresh dill**
salt
freshly ground black pepper

80 **fresh or preserved grape vine leaves**
water
1 **lemon, thinly sliced**
¼ **cup (2 fl oz/60 ml) olive oil**
lemon wedges and Yogurt (page 125) for
   serving

In a saucepan or frying pan with lid to fit, heat olive oil. Add onion and cook gently until transparent. Add rice and cook, stirring, for 5 minutes. Stir in pine nuts, currants, allspice, dill, and salt and pepper to taste. Cover and cook over gentle heat for 5 minutes. Remove pan from heat and set aside.

Working in 3 batches, blanch fresh or preserved grape vine leaves in boiling water for 2 minutes then transfer to a bowl of cold water. Drain well.

Spread 1 grape vine leaf on work surface shiny-side down, and place 1 heaping teaspoon filling toward stem end. Roll once, fold in sides and roll into a neat package. Repeat with remaining ingredients, reserving 8 vine leaves.

Line base of a large heavy-based saucepan with 4 grape vine leaves. Add prepared rolls, folded-side down, in closely packed rows in a single layer. As each row is completed, top with 3 slices lemon before beginning next row.

When all rolls have been placed in pan, top with 3 lemon slices and cover with remaining grape vine leaves. Pour 2 cups (16 fl oz/500 ml) water and olive oil over rolls, and invert a heavy plate on top to keep rolls in shape during cooking.

Bring to a slow simmer then reduce heat, cover and let simmer gently for 50 minutes. Remove pan from heat and let stand until cool.

Carefully transfer rolls to serving dish, discarding lemon slices. Serve at room temperature, or cover dish and refrigerate before serving. Garnish serving dish with lemon wedges, and serve with a bowl of yogurt.

Leek pie Pırasapide

Serves 6–8
Cooking time 30 minutes

1 quantity Hamur (Shortcrust Pastry) (page 18)
4–5 leeks
salt
1 cup (5 oz/150 g) crumbled beyaz peynir (feta
  cheese)
¼ cup (⅓ oz/10 g) finely chopped fresh flat-leaf
  (Italian) parsley
¼ teaspoon cayenne pepper
⅓ cup (3 fl oz/90 ml) olive oil
4 eggs

Make hamur according to directions on page 18, cover and set aside.

Remove roots and discolored leaves from leeks. Cut off most of green tops, leaving about 3 in (7.5 cm) intact. Cut leeks in half lengthways and wash well to remove soil between leaves. Cut out root core, then slice leeks fairly finely. If leeks are small, prepare more, as you will require 6–7 cups (1¼ lb/650 g) sliced leeks.

Place slices in a colander and wash again to ensure all soil has been removed. Drain well, then sprinkle with 1 tablespoon salt, rubbing it through leeks with your hands. Let stand until leeks are limp, 15–20 minutes, then press leeks well using the back of a spoon to extract moisture. Rinse briefly under cold running water and press again.

Combine leeks in a bowl with crumbled feta cheese, parsley, chili and oil. Beat eggs, reserve 2 teaspoons of beaten egg, and add remainder to leek mixture. Stir well to blend.

Divide hamur pastry in two pieces, with one piece slightly larger than the other. Roll out larger piece of pastry on a floured board, and place in a 12-in (30-cm) round baking dish or a 12- x 10-in (30- x 25-cm) baking dish.

Spread leek filling in pastry-lined baking dish and moisten pastry edge with water. Roll out remaining pastry and place on top. Press pastry together to seal well, then trim and crimp edge.

Beat reserved egg with a little milk and brush top of pastry. Cut small slits over surface with the point of a knife.

Bake in a preheated oven at 400–425°F (200–220°C/Gas 6–7) until golden-brown, about 30 minutes. Remove from oven and let stand for 10 minutes before cutting into serving portions.

NOTE: If desired, Yufka (Filo Pastry) (pages 28–9) may be used instead of hamur pastry. You will require 10 filo sheets in all. Line baking dish with 5 sheets, brushing each with melted butter before adding to dish. Add filling and top with remaining sheets, again brushing each with butter. Trim edges and butter top sheet. Score top layers lightly into serving portions using a sharp knife or razor blade. Sprinkle top lightly with water to prevent pastry from curling during cooking.

Fried cigarette pastries
Sıgara böreği

Makes 36
Cooking time About 1–1½ minutes each batch

12 sheets Yufka (Filo Pastry) (pages 28–9)
1 quantity meat or cheese filling (page 20)
water for sealing
oil for deep-frying

Open out filo pastry sheets, leave in a stack and, using a ruler and craft knife, cut stack into 3 strips, about 5 in (12 cm) wide and 12 in (30 cm) long. Stack on a clean kitchen towel and fold towel over top to cover.

Take 1 strip of pastry and place on work surface with narrow end toward you. Thinly spread about 2 teaspoons filling toward end, keeping ¾ in (2 cm) in from sides. Turn end of pastry over filling then fold in sides, pressing side folds along length of pastry. Lightly brush folded sides·and top end of pastry with water. Roll up firmly so that finished pastry is as slender as possible. Place seam-side down on a tray lined with a kitchen towel. Repeat with remaining ingredients.

Deep-fry pastries in batches, a few at a time, in hot oil, turning to brown evenly. Remove using a slotted spoon and drain on paper towels. Serve hot as an appetizer or as an accompaniment to light soups.

NOTE: Finished pastries may be reheated in a preheated oven at 350°F (180°C/Gas 4) if necessary.

Fried liver bits
Ciğer tavası

Serves 10–12
Cooking time 3–4 minutes for each batch

1 lb (500 g) lamb or calf liver
water
salt
all-purpose (plain) flour
olive oil for frying
freshly ground black pepper
½ cup (1½ oz/45 g) chopped scallions (shallots/spring onions)
¼ cup (⅓ oz/10 g) finely chopped fresh flat-leaf (Italian) parsley

Soak liver in enough salted water to cover for 30 minutes. Remove fine skin and larger tubes, and cut liver into ¾-in (2-cm) cubes. Drain well.

Toss liver cubes in flour to coat.

Add oil to a depth of ¼ in (5 mm) in a frying pan and heat well. Add only a single layer of liver cubes to pan at a time and cook quickly, turning with tongs to brown on all sides; take care not to overcook liver.

Using a slotted spoon, transfer to a serving dish then sprinkle with salt and pepper to taste. Top hot liver with chopped scallions and parsley, and serve immediately, providing toothpicks for your guests' convenience.

Poached eggs with yogurt and sage
Çılbır

Placing the yogurt in warmed dishes and topping it with hot eggs makes it warm enough for serving. Alternatively, you can top the eggs with yogurt. Don't place in a warm oven or the yogurt could separate.

Serves 4
Cooking time 4–5 minutes

1 cup (8 fl oz/250 ml) thick, country-style plain
   (natural) yogurt at room temperature
2 cloves garlic, pressed or crushed
1 teaspoon salt
8 eggs
vinegar, for poaching
¼ cup (2 oz/60 g) unsalted butter
½ teaspoon ground paprika
¼ teaspoon cayenne pepper
12 small fresh sage leaves
warm pita or crusty bread for serving

Combine yogurt, garlic and salt. Divide mixture between four warmed individual serving dishes or plates, spreading mixture evenly over bases.

Poach eggs in water with a little vinegar added.

Meanwhile, melt butter in a small frying pan. Add paprika, cayenne pepper and sage, and cook until butter sizzles, but do not let it burn. When eggs are poached as desired, remove with slotted spoon, drain, and place two in each dish. Pour a little sizzling butter mixture over each serving. Serve immediately with warm bread.

Filo pastry Yufka

Phyllo is the Greek name for this delicate, tissue-thin pastry, from the Greek word meaning "leaf." However, it is frequently spelt "filo." The Turks call the pastry "yufka."

Filo pastry is available commercially, either fresh (chilled) or frozen. If properly sealed, fresh pastry can be stored in the refrigerator for several weeks, but must never be frozen. Frozen filo pastry is more readily available at supermarkets. It varies slightly from fresh filo, a different formula being used to withstand the rigors of freezing. For thawing, follow the directions on the package. Both types of filo should be left in their packaging and brought to room temperature for 2 hours before using. If opened out while chilled, the pastry could break apart at the folds and can be difficult to handle.

HANDLING FILO PASTRY WHILE COOKING

Remove filo from packaging and open out. Spread sheets on a folded dry kitchen towel and cover with another folded dry kitchen towel. Moisten a third kitchen towel with water and wring it well to make it evenly damp. Spread over top cloth. Remove 1 filo sheet at a time, re-covering remaining filo with kitchen towels. If recipe requires pastry to be cut to size, cut all the sheets in a stack using a ruler and craft knife then stack again and cover. Filo dries out very quickly in the heat of the kitchen, so covering is essential, particularly if the shaping of individual pastries takes time.

HOMEMADE FILO PASTRY

Equipment required: Mixing bowl, rolling pin, wooden dowel no less than 24 in (60 cm) long and ¾ in (2 cm) in diameter, large work surface, large cloth and waxed (greaseproof) paper.

Sift 4 cups (1¼ lb/625 g) all-purpose (plain) flour and 1 teaspoon salt into mixing bowl. Add 1⅓ cups (11 fl oz/340 ml) tepid water with ¼ cup (2 fl oz/60 ml) olive, corn or peanut oil. Stir to a soft dough, then knead in bowl with hand for 10 minutes, using kneading action similar to bread making. It is easier to do this while sitting down with bowl placed in lap. Dough will feel sticky at first, but with kneading the gluten in the flour is developed and the dough becomes smooth and satiny.

When well-kneaded and smooth, wrap pastry in plastic wrap and let rest at room temperature for 1 hour or longer. Any dough not required for recipe may be wrapped in plastic wrap and stored in refrigerator for up to 1 week. Bring to room temperature before rolling out.

Divide pastry into 12 even portions, shaping each into a smooth ball. Cover with a kitchen towel.

Dust work surface lightly with flour. Take a ball of pastry and shape it into a square. Place on work surface and dust top with flour. Roll out to a 6-in (15-cm) square using a rolling pin. Dust again with flour. Take dowel and place on one end of pastry. Roll pastry neatly onto dowel, pressing firmly as you roll. Keep hands on each side of pastry. Unroll pastry and dust work surface and pastry again with flour. Roll up again from opposite side of pastry, again exerting even pressure. Unroll carefully. After second rolling, pastry should be about 10 x 12 in (25 x 30 cm) in size.

Using backs of hands (rings removed), place hands under pastry and stretch gently, moving hands to stretch it evenly, working toward edges. Edges can be given a final stretch with fingertips. You should end up with a piece of pastry about 14 x 18 in (35 x 45 cm) in size. Place on a kitchen towel, cover with waxed (greaseproof) paper and fold towel over pastry to cover. Repeat using remaining pastry, laying each completed sheet on top of previous one with paper in between.

Use soon after making, as directed in recipes; for pies and layered pastries where a number of sheets are required, use half the number of homemade filo sheets to those given in recipes.

Do not be concerned if the pastry tears during stretching. Tears may be mended as filo is being used, or avoided if cutting into pieces or strips.

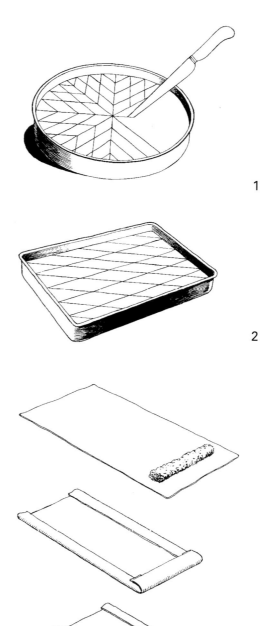

1

2

3

CUTTING AND SHAPING TECHNIQUES

Many recipes refer to cutting foods in diamond shapes for serving. This can be done whether the dish is round (see diagram 1), square or rectangular (see diagram 2).

The shaping of pastries in rolls, though described in recipes, is perhaps clarified with diagrams (see diagram 3).

soups

Wedding soup Düğün çorbası

Serves 6–8
Cooking time 2–2¼ hours

1 lb (500 g) boneless lamb stew meat
1 lb (500 g) lamb soup bones
8 cups (64 fl oz/2 L) water
1 onion, cut into quarters
1 carrot, cut into quarters
salt
freshly ground black pepper
⅓ cup (3 oz/90 g) butter
½ cup (2½ oz/75 g) all-purpose (plain) flour
3 egg yolks
2–3 tablespoons lemon juice
2 tablespoons melted butter for garnish
2 teaspoons paprika for garnish

Place lamb meat and soup bones in a large saucepan and add water, onion and carrot. Bring to a slow simmer, skimming when necessary. Add salt and pepper to taste, cover and simmer gently until lamb meat is tender, about 1½ hours.

Remove bones and discard. Lift out meat and cut into small pieces. Strain stock, return to pan and let simmer gently.

In another large saucepan, melt butter and stir in flour. Cook gently for 2 minutes; do not allow to color. Gradually add hot stock, stirring constantly. When soup is smooth and bubbling, let simmer gently.

Beat egg yolks in a bowl and gradually add lemon juice, reserving a little for seasoning. Gradually beat about 2 cups (16 fl oz/500 ml) soup into egg mixture, then pour mixture into soup. Stir over gentle heat and return lamb pieces to soup. Heat gently, stirring, until egg is cooked. Add lemon juice and salt to taste. Remove from heat.

Combine melted butter and paprika. Serve soup in deep bowls and garnish with a little butter-paprika mixture poured into center of each bowl.

Tripe soup Iskembe çorbası

Serves 5–6
Cooking time 2¼ hours

1 lb (500 g) tripe
water
1 small onion, cut into quarters
salt
white pepper
¼ cup (2 oz/60 g) butter
¼ cup (1½ oz/45 g) all-purpose (plain) flour
½ cup (4 fl oz/125 ml) milk
2 egg yolks
2 tablespoons lemon juice
2 teaspoons paprika
1 tablespoon oil
3–4 cloves garlic, crushed
⅓ cup (3 fl oz/90 ml) white wine vinegar

Wash tripe, place in a large saucepan with enough cold water to cover, and bring to a boil. Pour off cooking water from pan then add 5 cups (40 fl oz/1.25 L) cold water and onion, and return to heat. Add 2 teaspoons salt and white pepper to taste. Cover and simmer gently until tender, about 2 hours.

Remove onion and discard. Lift out tripe and cut into small strips. Reserve cooking liquid in pan.

Melt butter in a small saucepan and stir in flour. Cook for 1 minute; do not allow flour to color. Stir in milk and 3 cups (24 fl oz/750 ml) reserved cooking liquid. Stir constantly until thickened and bubbling, then let simmer gently over low heat.

In a mixing bowl, beat egg yolks then beat in lemon juice. Add to thickened stock, stirring constantly.

Return tripe strips to reserved cooking liquid in pan and add egg mixture, stirring constantly. Cook over gentle heat, stirring, until soup bubbles gently. Season to taste and remove from heat.

Mix paprika into oil and set aside.

Combine garlic and vinegar, and place into a small bowl for serving at the table.

Serve soup in individual bowls, garnished with a little paprika-oil floated on top. Garlic-vinegar mixture is added at the table according to individual taste.

Chilled yogurt and cucumber soup
Cacık

Cacık is Turkey's version of the yogurt and cucumber salad (Tzatziki) prepared in Greece and also in Lebanon, Syria, Cyprus. In Turkey, the mixture is also thinned down and, with a slight variation, presented as a soup. The cucumbers should be small and firm, with underdeveloped seeds.

Serves 6

2 small green cucumbers, peeled
salt
3 cups (24 fl oz/750 ml) plain (natural) yogurt
2 cloves garlic, pressed or crushed
2 tablespoons finely chopped fresh mint
1 tablespoon finely chopped fresh dill
   (optional)
3 tablespoons olive oil
about 1 cup (8 fl oz/250 ml) iced water
freshly ground white pepper
thin cucumber slices for garnish
fresh mint sprigs for garnish

Shred cucumber into colander and lightly mix in 1 teaspoon salt. Let stand in colander for 20 minutes to drain. Transfer to large bowl and add yogurt, garlic, mint, dill and olive oil. Cover and refrigerate at least 2 hours.

Just before serving, add iced water until soup is creamy but not too thin—amount depends on thickness of yogurt. Season with salt and pepper to taste. Garnish with cucumber slices and mint sprigs.

salads and vegetables

Beet salad
Pancar salatası

Serves 6–8

3 medium-sized cooked beets (beetroot)
2 cups (16 fl oz/500 ml) drained yogurt (page 125)
½ teaspoon caraway seeds
salt
freshly ground black pepper
1 tablespoon chopped fresh mint
fresh mint for garnish

Peel and cool beets if freshly cooked. Cut beets into ½-in (12-mm) cubes.

Reserve about ¼ cup beets and set aside. Mix remaining beets into yogurt with caraway seeds and salt and pepper to taste. Mix in mint. Cover and refrigerate to chill.

Place in serving bowl and garnish with reserved beets and mint leaves.

Eggplant salad
Patlıcan salatası

Serves 6–8
Cooking time 20 minutes

2 large, oval eggplants (aubergines), each about
    12 oz (375 g)
salt
½ cup (4 fl oz/125 ml) oil
2 cups (16 fl oz/500 ml) drained yogurt (page 125)
2 cloves garlic, crushed
salt
freshly ground black pepper
chopped walnuts for garnish (optional)

Cut eggplants in half lengthwise and then cut into slices ¼ in (5 mm) thick. Sprinkle slices liberally with salt (stack if necessary) and let stand for 30 minutes. Rinse and dry with paper towels.

Heat half of oil in a large frying pan, add eggplant and cook until golden brown on each side. Remove using a slotted spoon and drain on paper towels. Add more oil to pan as required.

Mix yogurt with crushed garlic and salt to taste.

Place a layer of cooled eggplant in serving dish, overlapping slices a little. Season with pepper and spread some yogurt on top. Repeat, finishing with a layer of yogurt. Cover and refrigerate. Serve garnished with chopped walnuts if desired.

NOTE: Eggplant salad may be layered in individual dishes for serving as a first course.

White bean salad Piyaz

Serves 6–8
Cooking time 2–2½ hours

2 cups (14 oz/440 g) dried haricot (navy) or
    other white beans
6 cups (48 fl oz/1.5 L) cold water
salt
1 clove garlic
2 small onions
¼ cup (2 fl oz/60 ml) lemon juice
1 tablespoon white wine vinegar
¼ cup (2 fl oz/60 ml) olive oil
¼ cup (2 fl oz/60 ml) good salad oil
¼ cup (⅓ oz/10 g) chopped fresh flat-leaf
    parsley
1 teaspoon chopped fresh mint
2 teaspoons chopped fresh dill

For serving:
1 green bell pepper (capsicum)
3 hard-cooked (boiled) eggs

Place beans in a bowl with cold water and soak overnight, in the refrigerator if weather is warm.

Drain soaked beans, place in a saucepan and add enough fresh water to cover. Bring to a boil, cover pan and simmer gently over low heat until beans are tender but still intact. Cooking time will vary according to bean used, but about 1½ hours should be sufficient. Add salt to taste after 1 hour. When beans are tender, drain well in colander or sieve, and transfer to a bowl.

Crush garlic with a little salt. Cut onions in half lengthwise then slice thinly into semicircles. Add onions to hot beans in bowl with lemon juice, vinegar and combined oils. Stir to combine then let stand until cool.

When salad has cooled, gently mix in chopped herbs. Refrigerate for 1–2 hours to chill.

Serve in a deep bowl, garnished with sliced green bell pepper and hard-cooked eggs sliced or cut into quarters.

Tomato salad Domates salatası

Serves 6–8

4 medium-sized, firm tomatoes
2 long, young cucumbers
¼ cup (2 fl oz/60 ml) lemon juice
1 tablespoon white vinegar
¼ cup (2 fl oz/60 ml) olive oil
1 teaspoon finely chopped fresh mint
1 tablespoon finely chopped fresh flat-leaf
   (Italian) parsley
salt
freshly ground black pepper
black olives, drained
parsley sprigs for garnish

Peel tomatoes if desired. Slice fairly thinly
and arrange in two rows on an oval platter.

Peel cucumbers and score with tines of
a fork. Slice thinly and arrange on one side
of tomatoes.

Beat together lemon juice, vinegar, oil
and herbs, and add salt and pepper to
taste. Pour over tomatoes and cucumbers.
Cover and refrigerate until required.

Just before serving, place olives on
other side of tomatoes and garnish platter
with parsley sprigs.

NOTE: This salad accompanies most
Turkish meals, particularly in summer
when tomatoes are at their best.

Swooning Imam Imam bayıldı

The story of the Imam swooning over this dish has been told so often that I shan't tell it again. Little did the man know that he would be immortalized through this most famous of eggplant dishes. There are versions of this dish in countries from Greece to Iran. It has always featured in Greek cuisine, with the claim that a Greek cook prepared it for the Imam while he lived in Greece. The truth will never be known!

Serves 4–8
Cooking time 1¼ hours

8 long (Japanese) eggplants (aubergines)
3 medium-sized onions
½ cup (4 fl oz/125 ml) olive oil
4 cloves garlic, chopped
3 medium-sized tomatoes, peeled
¼ cup (⅓ oz/10 g) chopped fresh flat-leaf
  (Italian) parsley
salt
freshly ground black pepper
2 tablespoons lemon juice
pinch sugar
½ cup (4 fl oz/125 ml) water

Remove stems from eggplants and wash well. Peel skin in ½-in (12-mm) strips lengthwise to get a striped effect. Cut a deep slit lengthwise on one side of each eggplant, stopping short of top and base. Long eggplants do not require salting.

Cut onions in half lengthwise then cut into slender wedges. In a heavy-based saucepan or frying pan with lid to fit, heat half of oil, add onion and cook gently until transparent. Add garlic, cook for 1 minute. Transfer onion and garlic to a bowl and combine with chopped tomatoes, parsley, and salt and pepper to taste.

Heat remaining oil in pan, add eggplants and cook over high heat until lightly browned all over but still rather firm. Remove pan from heat.

Arrange eggplants in pan so that slit faces up. Spoon filling mixture into slits, forcing in as much as possible. Spread remaining filling on top. Add lemon juice, sugar and water to pan, and cover tightly. Cook over gentle heat until tender, about 45 minutes. Add more water only if needed as eggplants release a lot of liquid.

Remove pan from heat and let cool to room temperature. Serve as an appetizer or as a light meal with bread, or refrigerate and serve chilled as an accompaniment.

Sultan's delight Hünkâr beğendi

Serves 6
Cooking time 40–50 minutes

1 lb (500 g) small eggplants (aubergines)
1 tablespoon lemon juice
¼ cup (2 oz/60 g) butter
¼ cup (1½ oz/45 g) all-purpose (plain) flour
¾ cup (6 fl oz/180 ml) milk
½ cup (1 oz/30 g) soft white breadcrumbs
   (optional)
½ cup (2 oz/60 g) grated kashkaval, kasseri or
   cheddar cheese
salt
freshly ground black pepper
finely chopped fresh parsley
Braised Lamb (Taş Kebapı) (page 84) for serving

Grill eggplant over glowing charcoal, or impale on a fork and hold over a gas flame, or place on electric hotplate on medium heat. Turn eggplant frequently until soft to touch and skin is charred to a certain degree. Alternatively, char skin only, then bake in a preheated 350°F (180°C/Gas 4) oven for 10–20 minutes, depending on size of eggplant.

Rinse off any burnt skin under cold running water, then peel off remaining skin. Puree eggplant in a blender or food processor, adding lemon juice as required to keep eggplant light in color.

Melt butter in a heavy-based saucepan and stir in flour. Cook gently for 2 minutes; do not allow flour to color. Add milk, stirring constantly until thickened and bubbling.

Add eggplant puree and cook over gentle heat until very thick and reduced a little, about 20 minutes. Stir occasionally. If desired, breadcrumbs may be stirred into puree to thicken it further.

Remove pan from heat. Add cheese and beat well until smooth, then season with salt and pepper to taste.

Pile puree around edge of serving dish, sprinkle with chopped parsley, and fill center with Braised Lamb. Or serve hot with roast lamb or chicken dishes.

NOTE: To prepare eggplant, you can also char the skin as described in recipe above then pierce skin in several places with a fine skewer and cook in microwave on High for 3–5 minutes, depending on size.

Vegetable casserole
Güveçte yaz türlüsü

Serves 6
Cooking time 1½–2 hours

2 long (Japanese) eggplants (aubergines) or
  1 medium-sized oval eggplant (aubergine)
salt
4 small zucchini (courgettes)
3 small green bell peppers (capsicums)
8 oz (250 g) okra (page 14) (optional)
8 oz (250 g) green beans
4–5 small ripe tomatoes, peeled
½ cup (4 fl oz/125 ml) olive oil
3 small onions, sliced
2 cloves garlic, crushed
¼ cup (⅓ oz/10 g) chopped fresh flat-leaf
  (Italian) parsley
freshly ground black pepper
½ cup (4 fl oz/125 ml) water

Remove stems from eggplants and wash well. Peel skin in ½-in (12-mm) strips lengthwise to get a striped effect. Cut long eggplants into ½-in (12 mm) slices; if using oval eggplant, cut into quarters lengthwise, then cut into chunky pieces. Spread eggplant on a tray and sprinkle liberally with salt. Let stand for 30 minutes, then pat dry with paper towels.

Trim zucchini and cut into 1½-in (4-cm) pieces. Remove stem and seeds from bell peppers and cut into quarters. Prepare okra as directed on page 14. String beans if necessary and cut in half (French cut). Slice tomatoes.

Heat half of oil in a frying pan, add eggplant and cook until lightly browned. Remove to a plate; do not drain.

Add remaining oil to pan, add sliced onions and cook gently until translucent. Stir in garlic and cook for 1 minute, then remove pan from heat.

Preheat oven to 350°F (180°C/Gas 4). Spread a layer of eggplant over base of a large baking dish (casserole dish). Top with some of zucchini, bell pepper and beans. Spread some onion mixture on top and cover with tomato slices. Sprinkle with salt, pepper and some of parsley. Repeat layering until all ingredients are used, reserving some tomato slices and parsley. Place prepared okra on top if using.

Finish with a layer of reserved tomato slices. Sprinkle with reserved parsley, and salt and pepper. Evenly pour water and oil reserved from cooking eggplant over dish.

Cover baking dish and bake in preheated oven until vegetables are tender, 1–1½ hours.

Serve from baking dish as an accompaniment to roast or grilled meats and poultry. Often, this casserole is served as a light meal, with bread and beyaz peynir (feta cheese).

Fried cauliflower
Karnabahar kızartması

Serves 6
Cooking time 25–30 minutes

1 medium-sized cauliflower
water
salt
juice of ½ lemon
2 eggs
freshly ground white pepper
fine dried breadcrumbs
oil for deepfrying

For serving:
Yogurt Sauce (Yogurt Salçası) (page 18)
 or Tarator (page 18)

Break cauliflower into florets and soak in enough salted water to cover, to release any insects. Rinse well.

Bring 6 cups (48 fl oz/1.5 L) water to a boil with lemon juice and 2 teaspoons salt. Add cauliflower and boil rapidly, uncovered, until just tender, 4–5 minutes.

Drain cauliflower in colander and spread out on paper towels to dry.

Beat eggs, and add white pepper and salt to taste. Dip cauliflower floret in egg, then roll in breadcrumbs to coat completely. Set aside on tray until all florets are prepared.

Deepfry florets in hot oil, a few at a time, turning to brown evenly. Using a slotted spoon, remove and drain on paper towels.

Serve hot as a vegetable accompaniment or as an appetizer with Yogurt Sauce or Tarator.

Chickpeas with spinach Nohutlu ıspanak

Serves 6
Cooking time 3 hours

1½ cups (9 oz/280 g) chickpeas (garbanzo beans)
water
¼ cup (2 fl oz/60 ml) olive oil
1 large onion, chopped
¼ cup (2 oz/60 g) tomato paste
1 teaspoon sugar
salt
freshly ground black pepper
1½ lb (750 g) spinach

Wash chickpeas well, place in a bowl, and cover with 4½ cups (36 fl oz/1.1 L) cold water. Let soak overnight, in a cool place if weather is hot.

Drain soaked chickpeas and place in a large saucepan with enough fresh water to cover. Bring to a boil, cover then reduce heat and simmer gently until tender, about 1½–2 hours. Remove pan from heat and set aside.

In a frying pan, heat oil and gently cook onion until translucent. Add tomato paste, sugar, and about 2 teaspoons salt and plenty of black pepper to taste. Stir onion mixture into cooked chickpeas.

Wash spinach well and remove roots, coarse stems and discolored leaves. Chop leaves and stems roughly.

Place pan of chickpeas over medium heat and add spinach in 4 batches. As each batch wilts, add another. When all spinach is added, cover pan and simmer gently for 15–20 minutes, adding more water only if necessary. Mixture should be moist, not too liquid.

Serve with bread, salad and pickles as a light meal. Also good served cold.

Braised leeks
Zeytinyağli pırasa

Serves 6
Cooking time 35–40 minutes

6 medium-sized leeks
½ cup (4 fl oz/125 ml) olive oil
1 medium-sized onion, sliced
2 tablespoons tomato paste
½ cup (4 fl oz/125 ml) water or light stock
¼ cup (⅓ oz/10 g) finely chopped fresh flat-leaf (Italian)
   parsley
½ teaspoon sugar
salt
freshly ground black pepper
juice of ½ lemon
1 teaspoon chopped fresh dill
fresh parsley or dill sprigs and lemon slices for garnish

Remove coarse outer leaves from leeks and trim roots even with base. Cut off most of green tops. Cut in half lengthwise and wash well to remove any soil. Drain.

Heat oil in a large saucepan or deep frying pan with lid to fit, add onions and cook gently until translucent. Add tomato paste mixed with water or stock, half of chopped parsley, sugar, and salt and pepper to taste. Bring to a boil, cover and simmer over low heat for 10 minutes.

Add leeks and lemon juice, spooning liquid in pan over leeks. Cover and simmer gently until leeks are tender, 15–20 minutes.

Transfer to a serving dish and sprinkle with remaining chopped parsley and chopped dill. Serve at room temperature or chilled, garnished with herb sprigs and lemon slices.

Braised carrots
Havuç pilakisi

Serves 6
Cooking time 35–40 minutes

1½ lb (750 g) medium-sized carrots
¼ cup (2 fl oz/60 ml) olive oil
2 medium-sized onions
1 cup (8 fl oz/250 ml) water
¼ cup (⅓ oz/10 g) finely chopped fresh flat-leaf (Italian)
   parsley
1 teaspoon sugar
salt
freshly ground black pepper
1 teaspoon lemon juice

Wash and scrape carrots. Cut diagonally into slices about ¼ in (5 mm) thick. Cut onions in half lengthwise, then slice into semicircles.

Heat oil in a large saucepan over medium heat, add onions and cook gently until translucent. Add carrots and cook for a further 5 minutes, stirring frequently.

Add water, half of parsley and sugar. Season with salt and pepper to taste. Cover pan tightly and simmer over low heat until tender, 15–20 minutes.

Stir in lemon juice and transfer to serving dish. Let cool at room temperature, or refrigerate to chill if desired, and serve sprinkled with remaining parsley. Serve as a vegetable accompaniment.

rice and grains

Pilaf Pilavlar

The pilavlar of Turkey have an established place in world cuisine; even so we have only been exposed to a few variations. The possible permutations and combinations of the pilaf are endless. The recipes given here are indicative of the various ways in which pilaf is prepared; once you have mastered pilaf cooking, you can devise your own variations.

The Turkish cook soaks the rice in hot, salted water for 10–30 minutes. With the rices available today, this is unnecessary. However, washing is necessary if you are to achieve the right result. Place rice in a bowl, add cold water and stir. Drain and add fresh water. Do this until water runs clear. Another method is to place rice in a sieve. Move the grains constantly with fingers so that the starch is released as the cold water runs through.

As rice grains vary in hardness according to the variety, you may find the directions given need slight modification for the type you are using. Perhaps you might require more or less liquid, and the cooking time may need to be extended or reduced. Make a note of any alterations necessary for that particular brand of rice.

To serve pilaf, either fluff up with a fork and pile on a serving dish, or press hot pilaf into an oiled mold and turn out onto a serving dish. A little of the sauce from the accompanying food may be spooned on top as additional garnish.

Spicy pilaf Iç pilavı

Serves 6
Cooking time 50 minutes

2 cups (14 oz/440 g) long-grain rice
8 oz (250 g) chicken or goose livers
⅓ cup (3 oz/90 g) butter
¼ cup (1½ oz/45 g) pine nuts
1 cup (3 oz/90 g) chopped scallions
   (shallots/spring onions), white part only
½ teaspoon ground cinnamon
¼ teaspoon ground allspice
¼ cup (1½ oz/45 g) currants
3 cups (24 fl oz/750 ml) chicken stock
salt
freshly ground black pepper
¼ cup (⅓ oz/10 g) finely chopped fresh flat-leaf
   (Italian) parsley or dill

Wash rice until water runs clear and drain using a sieve then let stand to drain completely.

Clean livers and slice finely or dice.

Heat half of butter in a small frying pan, add pine nuts and cook until golden. Remove using a slotted spoon and set aside on a plate.

Add scallions to butter in same pan and cook gently until soft. Add prepared liver and cook over medium heat until color changes; do not overcook. Stir in cinnamon and allspice, remove pan from heat and set aside.

In a deep, heavy-based saucepan over medium heat, heat remaining butter. Add drained rice and cook, stirring, until grains change from translucent to opaque without coloring. Stir in currants, then chicken stock, and salt and pepper to taste. Cook, stirring occasionally, until boiling then reduce heat to low, cover and simmer for 15 minutes.

Remove lid and add reserved pine nuts, scallion and liver mixture, and chopped parsley or dill. Stir gently through rice with a wooden spoon.

Place 2 paper towels over rim of pan and cover tightly with lid. Cook on very low heat for a further 20 minutes, using a heat diffuser if necessary. Remove pan from heat and let stand for 15 minutes before serving.

An excellent accompaniment for roast poultry or lamb.

Eggplant pilaf
Patlıcanlı pilavı

Serves 6
Cooking time 50 minutes

2 oval eggplants (aubergines), about 1 lb (500 g) in total
salt
1 large onion
⅓ cup (3 fl oz/90 ml) olive oil
2 cups (12 oz/375 g) chopped peeled tomatoes
1½ teaspoons salt
freshly ground black pepper
2 tablespoons chopped fresh flat-leaf (Italian) parsley
2 teaspoons chopped fresh mint
2 cups (14 oz/440 g) long-grain rice
2½ cups (20 fl oz/625 ml) light stock or water
yogurt for serving

Cut eggplants into large cubes with skin on. Place in a colander and sprinkle liberally with salt. Let stand for 30 minutes. Rinse and dry with paper towels.

Cut onion in half lengthwise, then cut into slices.

Heat ¼ cup (2 fl oz/60 ml) oil in a heavy-based frying pan, add eggplant cubes and cook until lightly browned. Remove from pan and set aside.

Heat remaining oil in pan, add onion and cook gently until translucent. Stir in tomatoes, salt, pepper, herbs and eggplant. Bring to a boil.

Wash rice until water runs clear then drain. Place on top of eggplant mixture and add stock or water. Bring to a boil without stirring. Reduce heat, cover pan and let simmer gently for 30 minutes.

Remove pan from heat. Remove lid, place 2 paper towels over rim of pan, replace lid tightly and let stand 10 minutes.

Stir gently and transfer to a heated serving dish. Serve with yogurt.

Turkistan carrot pilaf
Türkistan pilavı

Serves 5–6
Cooking time 30 minutes

2 cups (14 oz/440 g) long-grain rice
¼ cup (2 oz/60 g) butter
2 cups (12 oz/375 g) coarsely grated carrots
½ teaspoon whole black peppercorns
1 teaspoon sugar
3½ cups (28 fl oz/875 ml) chicken stock
salt

Wash rice until water runs clear. Drain well.

Heat butter in a heavy-based saucepan over medium heat, add grated carrot and peppercorns, and cook for 3 minutes, stirring often. Sprinkle in sugar toward end of cooking.

Add rice and cook for a further 2 minutes, stirring constantly.

Pour in stock and add salt to taste. Bring to a boil, stirring, then reduce heat to low. Cover and cook over low heat for 25–30 minutes. Remove pan from heat. Remove lid, place 2 paper towels over rim of pan, replace lid tightly, and let stand 10 minutes.

Excellent with roast chicken or Chicken in Pastry (Tavuk Yufka İçinde) (page 79).

Pilaf in pastry Yufkali iç pilavı

Serves 8–10
Cooking time 1½ hours

For pilaf:
¼ cup (2 oz/60 g) butter
½ cup (2½ oz/75 g) split or slivered almonds
1 large onion, finely chopped
1 cup (6 oz/185 g) coarsely grated carrot
8 oz (250 g) lean boneless lamb, cut in ½-in (1-cm) cubes
1 cup (6 oz/185 g) chopped dried apricots
1 teaspoon ground allspice
1½ teaspoons salt
freshly ground black pepper
3½ cups (28 fl oz/875 ml) water or light stock
2 cups (14 oz/440 g) long-grain rice
1 cup (2½ oz/75 g) crumbled vermicelli noodles

6–8 sheets Yufka (Filo Pastry) (pages 28–9)
   or 1 quantity Hamur (Shortcrust Pastry) (page 18)
⅓–½ cup (3–4 fl oz/90–125 ml) melted butter

In a large saucepan, heat half of butter, add almonds and cook until golden. Remove using slotted spoon and set aside.

Heat remaining butter in pan, add onion and cook gently until translucent. Stir in carrot and cook a further 5 minutes.

Increase heat, add lamb cubes and cook, stirring, until lamb changes color. Stir in apricots, allspice, salt, and plenty of pepper to taste. Add 1 cup (8 fl oz/250 ml) water or stock, stir then reduce heat, cover and simmer gently for 15 minutes.

Meanwhile, wash rice until water runs clear then drain well.

Add remaining water or stock to pan and bring to a boil. Stir in noodles and drained rice. Bring to a boil over medium heat, stirring occasionally. Cover and reduce heat to low. Cook gently until liquid is absorbed and rice is just tender, about 20 minutes. Remove from heat and let stand; keep covered.

Preheat oven to 375°F (190°C/Gas 5). Grease an 8-cup (64-fl oz/2-L) pudding basin or square baking dish (casserole dish) with melted butter.

Brush 1 filo sheet with melted butter, top with another sheet, and set aside. Continue buttering the remaining sheets in pairs in the same way. You will require 3 pairs of buttered sheets for a pudding basin, 4 for a square baking dish.

Place 1 pair of sheets in prepared dish, positioning it across base and up sides, with end of pastry generously overhanging edge of dish; there should be enough to fold pastry back over top of dish. Butter pastry in dish then arrange remaining pastry in the same way so that dish is covered with pastry and with enough overlap. If using hamur pastry, roll out pastry sheet to fit dish with enough overlap to cover finished pie.

Add almonds to pilav in pan and stir to combine. Spoon pilav into pastry-lined dish, spreading top evenly. Pour ¼ cup (2 fl oz/60 ml) melted butter evenly over pilav. Fold pastry over pilav to cover, brushing top of each sheet with butter as it is put into place. Brush top with butter. Bake in preheated oven for 30 minutes.

Invert onto serving platter and cut into wedges. Serve as a light meal, as part of a buffet, or as a first course.

White pilaf
Beyaz pilavı

Serves 6
Cooking time 35 minutes

2 cups (14 oz/440 g) long-grain rice
¼ cup (2 oz/60 g) butter
3½ cups (28 fl oz/875 ml) chicken stock
salt

Wash rice until water runs clear then drain well.

Heat butter in a large heavy-based saucepan over medium heat, add drained rice and cook, stirring, for 5 minutes.

Add stock and salt to taste, and cook, stirring occasionally, until boiling. Reduce heat, cover and let simmer for 20 minutes. Test a grain to gauge when cooked; it should be firm to bite but evenly tender.

Remove pan from heat. Remove lid, place 2 paper towels over rim of pan, replace lid tightly, and let stand for 10 minutes. It may be left for as long as 30 minutes without spoiling, depending of course on the quality of the grain.

Fluff up with a fork and serve, or spoon into an oiled mold, press firmly and unmold onto serving dish.

Wedding pilaf
Düğün pilavı

Follow White Pilaf recipe, adding ¼ cup (1½ oz/45 g) pine nuts or blanched pistachio nuts when cooking rice in butter. Use meat stock in place of chicken stock.

Tomato pilaf
Domateslı pilavı

Follow White Pilaf recipe, adding 1½ cups (9 oz/280 g) chopped, peeled tomatoes halfway through cooking rice in butter. Use chicken or meat stock, as desired, reducing quantity to 2½ cups (20 fl oz/625 ml) if canned tomatoes have been used. Season with salt and pepper to taste.

Bulgur pilaf Bulgur pilavı

The traditional Turkish recipe uses meat or chicken stock; however, vegetable stock or water may be used for vegetarian cooking.

Serves 6
Cooking time 40 minutes

1 green bell pepper (capsicum)
1 large ripe tomato, peeled
¼ cup (2 oz/60 g) butter
1 medium onion, finely chopped
2 cups (12 oz/375 g) coarse bulgur (burghul)
3 cups (24 fl oz/750 ml) chicken stock or water
1 tablespoon chopped fresh mint
salt and freshly ground black pepper
plain (natural) yogurt for serving (optional)

Remove seeds from bell pepper and tomato and cut into pieces.

Melt butter in a large saucepan or deep frying pan with lid to fit, add onion and cook gently, stirring often, until translucent, about 10 minutes. Add bell pepper pieces, stir and cook a further 2–3 minutes. Add bulgur and cook, stirring often, a further 4 minutes. Stir in tomato, stock, mint, and salt and pepper to taste, and bring to a boil. Stir then reduce heat, cover and simmer gently until liquid is absorbed, about 20 minutes.

Remove pan from heat. Remove lid, place 2 paper towels over rim of pan, replace lid tightly and let stand 10 minutes.

Fluff up bulgur with fork. Serve with bowl of yogurt, if desired.

White bean stew Fasulye pilakisi

Serves 6–8
Cooking time 2–2½ hours

2 cups (14 oz/440 g) dried haricot (navy) beans
   or other small white beans
6 cups (48 fl oz/1.5 L) water
½ cup (4 fl oz/125 ml) olive oil
2 large onions, chopped
2 cloves garlic, chopped
1 cup (5 oz/150 g) diced carrot
1 cup (4 oz/125 g) sliced celery including leaves
¼ cup (2 oz/60 g) tomato paste
½ teaspoon sugar
pinch cayenne pepper
juice of ½ lemon
salt
¼ cup (⅓ oz/10 g) chopped fresh parsley

Wash beans in several changes of cold water and drain. Place in a large saucepan with water and bring to a boil. Boil for 2 minutes then remove pan from heat, cover and let stand until beans are plump, about 2 hours.

In a frying pan, heat oil. Add onion and cook gently until transparent. Add garlic, carrot and celery, and cook, stirring often, for 5 minutes. Remove pan from heat and set aside.

Return beans to a boil and boil gently, covered, for 30 minutes. Stir in cooked vegetables, tomato paste, sugar and cayenne pepper. Cover and simmer until beans are tender without being broken, about 1½ hours.

Stir in lemon juice, salt to taste and half of parsley. Cook for a further 10 minutes. Transfer to a deep dish for serving and sprinkle with remaining parsley. May be served hot or cold.

Spinach and eggs Ispanaklı yumurta

Serves 2 as a luncheon dish, 4 as
a first course
Cooking time 20–25 minutes

1½ lb (750 g) fresh spinach or 8-oz (250-g)
   package frozen spinach
1 medium-sized onion, finely chopped
2 tablespoons butter
⅓ cup (1½ oz/45 g) coarsely crumbled beyaz
   peynir (feta cheese)
salt
freshly ground black pepper
4 eggs

Clean fresh spinach, removing roots, coarse stems and discolored leaves. Wash leaves and stems well, shake off excess water and shred. If using frozen spinach, follow directions below.

In a frying pan with lid to fit, melt butter over medium heat. Add onion and cook gently until translucent. Add shredded fresh spinach and cook, stirring, until leaves wilt and liquid runs. Continue to cook until just enough liquid to cover base of pan remains. If using frozen spinach, add to pan with cooked onions, cover and place over low heat. Turn occasionally until thawed then bring to a simmer.

Season with salt and pepper and stir in crumbled cheese.

Make 4 depressions in spinach mixture and break 1 egg into each. Cover frying pan and cook over medium heat until eggs are set. Serve immediately.

NOTE: To serve attractively as a first course, divide spinach mixture into 4 individual ovenproof dishes and heat in a preheated 350°F (180°C/Gas 4) oven. Add eggs, drizzle a little melted butter over each, and bake until set.

Vegetable omelet Menemen

Serves 4
Cooking time 20–25 minutes

1 green bell pepper (capsicum)
1 red bell pepper (capsicum)
1 large onion
¼ cup (2 oz/60 g) butter
   or ¼ cup (2 fl oz/60 ml) oil
1 cup (6 oz/185 g) chopped, peeled tomatoes
salt
freshly ground black pepper
6 eggs
½ cup (2½ oz/75 g) crumbled beyaz peynir (feta cheese)
¼ cup (⅓ oz/10 g) chopped fresh flat-leaf (Italian) parsley

Cut peppers in half lengthwise, remove stem, seeds and white membrane. Cut into short strips. Cut onion in half lengthwise then slice into semicircles.

Heat butter or oil in a large frying pan over medium heat, add peppers and onion, and cook, stirring often, until onion is translucent.

Add tomatoes, salt and pepper to taste, and bring to a boil. Simmer gently until vegetables are soft, 3–4 minutes.

Beat eggs lightly, pour into pan and stir gently into vegetables until eggs set in creamy curds. Gently fold in cheese and most of parsley, reserving 1 tablespoon parsley for garnish.

Serve immediately with remaining parsley sprinkled on top.

Skewered swordfish Kılıç şiş

Serves 6
Cooking time 10–12 minutes

2 lb (1 kg) swordfish

For marinade:
¼ cup (2 fl oz/60 ml) lemon juice
2 tablespoons olive oil
1 small onion, sliced
1 teaspoon paprika
1 teaspoon salt
freshly ground black pepper
2 bay leaves, crumbled

For Lemon Sauce (Limon Salçası):
¼ cup (2 fl oz/60 ml) olive oil
¼ cup (2 fl oz/60 ml) lemon juice
¼ cup (⅓ oz/10 g) finely chopped fresh flat-leaf
  (Italian) parsley
salt
freshly ground black pepper

White Pilaf (Beyaz Pilavı) (page 52) for serving

When purchasing swordfish, ask for it to be cut 1¼ in (3 cm) thick. Remove skin if present, and cut fish into 1¼-in (3-cm) cubes.

Combine marinade ingredients in a glass or ceramic bowl. Add fish, turn to coat with marinade, cover and refrigerate for 1–2 hours, turning fish occasionally.

Thread fish onto 6 skewers and cook over glowing charcoal for 10–12 minutes, turning skewers frequently and brushing occasionally with marinade.

To make Lemon Sauce: Combine all ingredients in a screwtop jar, seal tightly and shake.

Serve hot skewered fish with White Pilaf, with sauce served separately.

NOTE: Lemon Sauce (Limon Salçası) is used as a dressing for grilled, fried, boiled and baked fish, salads and vegetables.

Baked fish Balık pilakisi

Serves 6
Cooking time 1 hour

6 fish steaks
salt
freshly ground black pepper
2 medium-sized onions
⅓ cup (3 fl oz/90 ml) olive oil
2 cloves garlic, finely chopped
½ cup (2½ oz/75 g) chopped celery, including
  leaves
½ cup (2 oz/60 g) thinly sliced carrot
1½ cups (9 oz/280 g) chopped, peeled
  tomatoes
½ cup (4 fl oz/125 ml) water
lemon slices and chopped fresh parsley for
  serving

Season fish with salt and pepper. Cover and set aside while preparing sauce.

Cut onions in half lengthwise, then slice into semicircles. In a frying pan, heat oil. Add onion, garlic, celery and carrot, and cook gently until onion is translucent. Add tomatoes and water, and season to taste with salt and pepper. Cover and simmer gently for 20 minutes.

Spoon some of sauce over base of a baking dish. Add fish steaks and top with remaining sauce. Bake in a preheated oven at 350°F (180°C/Gas 4) until fish flakes easily with a fork, about 30 minutes. Serve hot or cold.

Fish balls
Balık köftesi

Serves 8–10 as an appetizer
Cooking time 6–8 minutes each batch

For fish balls:
1½ lb (750 g) fish fillets
½ cup (1½ oz/45 g) chopped scallions (shallots/spring
   onions)
¼ cup (⅓ oz/10 g) chopped fresh flat-leaf (Italian) parsley
1 teaspoon chopped fresh dill
1½ cups (3 oz/90 g) soft white breadcrumbs
1 egg
salt
freshly ground black pepper

all-purpose (plain) flour for coating
oil for deep-frying
lemon wedges for serving

Skin fillets and remove any bones. Chop roughly and combine with scallions, parsley and dill.

Put fish mixture through food grinder using fine screen, or process to a paste in a food processor in 2 batches.

Transfer to a mixing bowl and add breadcrumbs, egg, and about 1 teaspoon salt and pepper to taste. Mix to a firm paste, adding a little more breadcrumbs if necessary, depending on type of fish used.

With moistened hands, shape mixture into walnut-sized balls. Refrigerate to firm if time allows.

Coat balls with flour and, working in batches of about 8 at a time, deep-fry in hot oil for 6–8 minutes, turning to brown evenly. Using a slotted spoon, transfer to drain on paper towels.

Serve hot with lemon wedges.

Fish steamed in paper Kagitta balık bugulamasi

Serves 4
Cooking time 20 minutes

olive oil
4 scallions (shallots/spring onions), chopped
3 tablespoons chopped fresh flat-leaf (Italian) parsley
4 thick fish steaks, such as swordfish, ling, blue-eye cod or
   sea bass, each about 8 oz (250 g)
salt
juice of ½ lemon
1 tablespoon butter
lemon wedges for serving

Preheat oven to 375°F (190°C/Gas 5). Tear 4 squares of baking (parchment) paper off a roll and place on work surface. Brush center of each with olive oil.

Combine scallions with parsley and divide in half. Using one half of herb mixture, spread onto oiled center of each paper and top with 1 fish steak. Season with salt and drizzle with a little lemon juice. Top with remaining herb mixture, evenly divided between each parcel, and a little knob of butter.

To wrap, bring sides of paper over fish and make a double fold. Fold in ends as if wrapping a parcel, and tuck folded ends underneath. Place on a baking sheet. Repeat with remaining parcels. Brush each parcel lightly with water to prevent paper scorching. Bake for 20 minutes.

Transfer parcels to serving plates and garnish with lemon wedges.

Sardines in grape vine leaves
Sardalya sarması

The leaves of the grape vine are used extensively in Turkey for wrapping food. They are particularly good wrapped around fish then broiled (grilled) or cooked on the barbecue, and impart a particular fragrance as well as keeping the fish moist. Besides fresh sardines, red mullet (goatfish) can also be prepared in this way. The leaves are removed before eating.

Serves 4
Cooking time 6 minutes

2 lb (1 kg) fresh sardines (about 24)
½ cup (4 fl oz/125 ml) olive oil
salt
24 fresh or preserved grape vine leaves
½ lemon
freshly ground black pepper

For serving:
lemon wedges
extra virgin olive oil
crusty bread

Leave sardines whole or cut off heads as desired. Remove fins from belly. Cut lengthwise from head, if retained, almost to tail and remove intestines, removing gills as well. Rinse well, drain and pat dry with paper towels.

Place sardines in dish, drizzle with half of oil and sprinkle lightly with salt. Toss lightly to distribute oil, cover and refrigerate at least 30 minutes.

Meanwhile, blanch fresh or preserved vine leaves in boiling water for 1 minute. Drain in colander, rinse under cold running water, and set aside to drain well.

Place vine leaf, shiny-side down, on work surface and place sardine across stem end. Squeeze on a little lemon juice and season with pepper. Roll up to top of leaf leaving head exposed if retained. Arrange on rack of broiler (grill) pan.

When all rolls are completed, brush all over with olive oil and broil (grill) until leaves begin to scorch, about 3 minutes each side. Alternatively, wrapped sardines may be arranged in a hinged barbecue grid and cooked on barbecue.

Serve hot with lemon wedges, small pitcher of olive oil and crusty bread.

Poached sea bass with almond sauce
Badem taratorlu levrek

Fish simply poached becomes something special when served with a creamy garlic sauce called tarator. Almonds are used in this recipe, but hazelnuts, walnuts or pine nuts can replace them (see page 18). Fish suitable for this dish are sea bass, blue-eyed cod, sole or halibut. A cool salad makes a perfect accompaniment. Any leftover tarator can be covered and stored in the refrigerator for up to a month.

Serves 6
Cooking time 6–8 minutes

6 fish fillets or steaks
2 cups (16 fl oz/500 ml) water
salt
¼ teaspoon black peppercorns
1 tablespoon lemon juice
1 bay leaf
2 sprigs fresh flat-leaf (Italian) parsley

Rinse fish and pat dry with paper towels.

Pour water into a large frying pan with lid to fit. Add salt to taste, peppercorns, lemon juice, bay leaf and parsley, cover and bring to a boil. Boil for 10 minutes. Add fish, and more water to just cover if necessary, then reduce heat, cover and simmer until fish flakes when tested with knife point, about 6–8 minutes. Let cool in cooking liquid.

To serve, lift fish out of liquid and drain well. Place on individual plates and spoon over Almond Sauce to mask fish. Serve with a light dusting of paprika, if desired.

Almond Sauce (Tarator)

1 cup (2 oz/60 g) soft white breadcrumbs
1 cup (4 oz/125 g) ground blanched almonds
2 cloves garlic
3 tablespoons lemon juice
4–6 tablespoons cold water
¼ cup (2 fl oz/60 ml) olive oil
salt
paprika for serving (optional)

Place breadcrumbs, almonds, garlic, lemon juice and 4 tablespoons water in a food processor, and process until thick and smooth. With motor running, gradually add oil in a thin stream. Add salt to taste and extra water if necessary to make a thick creamy sauce.

Sea bass in paper Kagıtta levrek

Sea bass is one of the most popular fish in Turkey. It is served here wrapped in a rather basic manner—not the heart-shaped paper cases of the French *en papillote* method, but just as effective. Aluminum foil is given as an alternative, but it does not puff up like paper, nor allow some of the steam to escape during cooking. If using foil, place fish on the shiny side so the dull side ends up as the outside of the parcel. Place cooked parcels on warm dinner plates to be opened at the table.

Serves 6
Cooking time 25 minutes

6 sea-bass fillets or other firm, white-fleshed
   fish fillets, about 7 oz (220 g) each
salt and freshly ground black pepper
½ cup (4 oz/125 g) butter, melted
1 lemon, halved
6 small bay leaves
6 small sprigs fresh thyme
6 small sprigs fresh flat-leaf (Italian) parsley
4 scallions (shallots/spring onions), julienned
4 medium tomatoes, peeled and sliced

Preheat oven to 375–400°F (190–200°C/ Gas 5–6). Season fish lightly with salt and pepper. Cut 6 sheets parchment (baking) paper or aluminum foil, each large enough to wrap a fish fillet. Brush center of each sheet with a little melted butter. Place 1 fish fillet in center of each sheet and squeeze a little lemon juice over. Top each fillet with 1 bay leaf, 1 thyme sprig, 1 parsley sprig and some scallions. Drizzle with more melted butter and arrange tomato slices on top to cover fish. Season with salt and pepper, and drizzle with more melted butter.

To wrap, bring sides of paper together and triple-fold across top. Twist paper at each end, or double-fold foil to seal. Place parcels in single layer on a baking sheet or in shallow baking dish. If using paper, sprinkle parcels with cold water.

Bake for 25 minutes then serve immediately.

Stuffed mussels Midye dolması

Serves 8–10
Cooking time 1 hour

For filling:
⅓ cup (3 fl oz/90 ml) olive oil
1 large onion, finely chopped
¼ cup (1½ oz/45 g) pine nuts
⅔ cup (4½ oz/140 g) long-grain rice, washed
2 tablespoons chopped fresh flat-leaf (Italian)
   parsley
½ teaspoon ground allspice
1 cup (6 oz/185 g) chopped peeled tomatoes
salt
freshly ground black pepper

40 large mussels
1 cup (8 fl oz/250 ml) water or fish stock
lemon slices or wedges, and fresh parsley
   sprigs for serving
Tarator (page 18) for serving

Heat oil in a saucepan or frying pan with lid to fit, add onion and gently cook until translucent. Add pine nuts, stir and cook for 2 minutes. Stir in rice, parsley, allspice, tomatoes and their liquid, and season with salt and pepper to taste. Cover and let simmer gently until liquid is absorbed, about 15 minutes.

Prepare mussels (see note below).

Place 1–2 heaping teaspoons filling in each mussel and re-close the shell as much as possible. Arrange in a large heavy-based saucepan in even layers. Invert a heavy plate on top to keep mussels closed.

Add water or stock to saucepan, bring to a simmer, cover and simmer gently for 30 minutes. Remove pan from heat and let stand until cool.

Lift out mussels and wipe each with paper towels. Shells may be lightly oiled for a more attractive appearance. Arrange on a serving dish, and garnish with lemon and parsley sprigs. Serve with Tarator. If not required for immediate use, place mussels in refrigerator. They can be served chilled or at room temperature.

NOTE: To prepare mussels, scrub well with a stiff brush, scraping shell with a knife to remove any marine growth. Tug beard toward pointed end to remove. To open easily, place scrubbed mussels in warm salted water. As they open, insert point of knife between the 2 shells and slide it toward pointed end to sever the closing mechanism. For stuffing, do not separate shells; shells may be separated if removing mussel meat for other recipes.

Fried brislings or sprats
Hamsi kızartması

Serves 6 as an appetizer
Cooking time 2 minutes each batch

1 lb (500 g) brislings, sprats or other tiny fish
salt
all-purpose (plain) flour
1 cup (8 fl oz/250 ml) oil for frying
fresh parsley sprigs and lemon slices for
  garnish
Lemon Sauce (Limon Salçası) (page 60) for
  serving

Wash and drain fish; there is no need to
clean insides unless you prefer to do so.
Leave fish intact. Drain, sprinkle with salt,
and let stand for 10 minutes.

Coat fish with flour. Taking 4 or 5 fish at
a time, moisten tails with water and press
tails together to form a fan, dusting tails
again with flour.

Heat oil in a frying pan, add fish and
cook until golden-brown and crisp, about
1 minute each side. Using a slotted spoon,
remove to drain on paper towels.

Serve hot, garnished with parsley and
lemon slices, and with a bowl of Lemon
Sauce on the side.

Fried mussels Midye tavası

Traditionally mussels are rolled in flour, then dipped in beer. The modern Turk has combined the two to make this crisp, light batter—so much simpler and less messy—and the result is delicious.

Serves 6
Cooking time 15–20 minutes

For beer batter:
1 cup (5 oz/150 g) all-purpose (plain) flour
1 teaspoon salt
about ¾ cup (6 fl oz/180 ml) beer

40 mussels (see Note, page 72)
all-purpose (plain) flour for coating
oil for deep-frying
lemon wedges and fresh parsley sprigs for
  serving
Tarator (page 18) for serving

To make beer batter: Sift flour and salt into a mixing bowl. Pour in beer and mix to a smooth batter, adding a little more beer if necessary.

If mussels are in shells, prepare as directed in note on page 72, and remove mussel meat from shells with point of a knife. Drain mussels on paper towels.

Toss mussels in flour to coat lightly. Working with a few at a time, dip in batter and deep-fry in hot oil, turning to brown evenly. Using a slotted spoon, remove and drain on paper towels.

Serve hot, garnishing platter with lemon and parsley. Serve Tarator in a bowl alongside and provide toothpicks for eating.

Circassian chicken Çerkez tavugu

Serves 6
Cooking time 2 hours

1 chicken, about 3 lb (1.5 kg)
1 large onion, cut into quarters
1 carrot, cut into quarters
2 sprigs fresh flat-leaf (Italian) parsley
3 cups (24 fl oz/750 ml) cold water
salt
freshly ground white pepper
3 slices stale white bread, crusts removed
1½ cups (6 oz/185 g) finely ground walnuts
½ teaspoon paprika
1 clove garlic, crushed, optional

For serving:
½ teaspoon paprika
1 tablespoon walnut oil
finely chopped fresh parsley (optional)

Place chicken in a medium-sized saucepan with onion, carrot, parsley and water. Bring to a slow simmer, skimming as necessary. Season with about 1½ teaspoons salt and pepper to taste. Cover and simmer very gently for 1½ hours; do not boil as this makes flesh stringy.

Let cool a little, then transfer chicken to a plate. Remove meat then set aside, and return skin and bones to saucepan. Boil stock with bones and skin until reduced by half. Strain and reserve stock.

Cut chicken meat into 2-in (5-cm) strips and place in a bowl. Moisten with 2 tablespoons stock, cover and refrigerate.

Soak bread in a little stock, squeeze and crumble into a bowl. Add walnuts, paprika and garlic if using. Combine and put through a food grinder using fine screen, or process in a food processor or blender.

Slowly beat in 1 cup (8 fl oz/250 ml) warm chicken stock, adding a little more if necessary to make a smooth, thick sauce. Adjust seasoning with salt and pepper.

Mix one-third of walnut sauce gently into chicken. Arrange chicken mixture into an attractive mound on a shallow dish and spread remaining sauce over it. Cover lightly with plastic wrap and refrigerate.

Steep paprika in walnut oil to color oil, 10 minutes or longer. Drizzle over chicken just before serving. Garnish with chopped parsley if desired. Serve cold with salad accompaniments.

NOTE: Walnut oil is obtainable from some gourmet food and health food stores.

Chicken in filo Tavuk yufka içinde

Serves 6
Cooking time 45 minutes

⅓ **cup (3 oz/90 g) butter**
2 lb (1 kg) chicken breast fillets
4 small onions
1 large ripe tomato, peeled
salt
freshly ground black pepper
¾ **cup (6 fl oz/180 ml) water**

12 sheets Yufka (Filo Pastry) (pages 28–9)
⅓ **cup (3 fl oz/90 ml) melted butter**
fresh parsley sprigs for garnish

Heat half of butter in a frying pan over medium heat and add chicken. Cook, turning frequently to brown all over, until just cooked through, about 10 minutes. Remove to a plate.

Cut onions in half lengthwise and slice thinly into semicircles. Add to pan with remaining butter and cook gently until transparent. Chop tomato and add to pan with salt and pepper to taste. Stir in water and cook gently until moisture evaporates. Mixture should look oily.

Cut breasts into strips about 2 in (5 cm) long and add to pan. Stir gently to combine then remove pan from heat.

Preheat oven to 375°F (190°C/Gas 5).

Spread out 1 sheet filo pastry, brush with melted butter and place another sheet on top. Brush top with butter and fold pastry in half to give almost a square shape. Cover with kitchen towel. Repeat with remaining pastry.

Take a square of pastry and place one-sixth filling in center, slightly toward one corner. Fold this corner over filling then fold adjacent corners on top and finish like a parcel, tucking last corner underneath parcel. Place on lightly buttered baking sheet. Repeat with remaining ingredients.

Brush top of each parcel lightly with melted butter and bake until golden, about 15 minutes. Serve immediately, garnishing with parsley sprigs. Turkistan Carrot Pilaf (Türkistan Pilavı) (page 49) is a good accompaniment.

Chicken casserole with okra
Piliçli bamya güveci

Serves 4
Cooking time 1 hour

1 lb (500 g) okra
1 teaspoon salt
½ cup (4 fl oz/125 ml) distilled white vinegar
2 young chickens (poussins), about 1½ lb
  (750 g) each
2 tablespoons olive oil
2 tablespoons butter
1 onion, finely chopped
1 clove garlic, pressed or crushed
14 oz (425 g) can tomatoes, chopped, with
  liquid
1 tablespoon tomato paste
1 teaspoon sugar
½ cup (4 fl oz/125 ml) water
1 bay leaf
freshly ground black pepper
finely chopped fresh parsley, to serve

Trim stalk tips from okra, and trim carefully around conical tops of stalks to remove fibrous layer, taking care not to cut into pods. Dissolve 1 teaspoon salt in vinegar in a large bowl. Add okra and turn mixture using your hands. Let stand 30 minutes. Drain in colander and rinse well.

Cut chickens in half, rinse and dry with paper towels. Heat oil and butter in large, wide saucepan. Add chicken and cook until browned all over, about 3 minutes each side. Remove chicken to a plate.

Reduce heat, add onion to pan and cook gently until transparent, about 5 minutes. Stir in garlic and cook for several seconds. Add tomatoes with their liquid, tomato paste, sugar, water, bay leaf, and salt and pepper to taste. Return chicken to pan, turn to coat in sauce, cover and simmer gently for 20 minutes.

Place okra carefully on top of chicken in pan; it should not be covered with sauce. Cover and simmer until okra and chicken are tender, about 20 minutes.

Remove okra with slotted spoon to warm dish. Lift chicken onto serving platter, pour sauce over and arrange okra around chicken. Sprinkle with chopped parsley before serving.

Serve with steamed rice or pilaf.

Lamb in filo Talaş kebapı

Serves 4
Cooking time 1¾ hours

1½ lb (750 g) boneless lamb from shoulder
2 tablespoons butter
1 small onion, finely chopped
1 cup (6 oz/185 g) chopped peeled tomatoes
2 tablespoons chopped fresh flat-leaf (Italian)
  parsley
salt
freshly ground black pepper

8 sheets Yufka (Filo Pastry) (pages 28–9)
⅓ cup (3 fl oz/90 ml) melted butter

Trim lamb and cut into ½-in (1-cm) cubes.

Heat butter in a large saucepan, add lamb and cook over high heat, stirring often, to brown all over. Reduce heat to medium, add onion and cook for a further 10 minutes, stirring occasionally.

Stir in tomatoes and parsley, and season with salt and pepper to taste. Cover and simmer gently for 1 hour. Increase heat to reduce liquid to a thick sauce if necessary. Remove pan from heat.

Preheat oven to 350–375°F (180–190°C/Gas 4–5). Grease or butter a baking sheet.

Spread out 1 sheet filo pastry, brush with melted butter and place another sheet on top. Brush top with butter and fold pastry in half to give almost a square shape. Cover with kitchen towel. Repeat with remaining pastry.

Take 1 square of pastry and brush top with butter. Spread one-fourth of lamb mixture toward one end, leaving sides clear. Fold end of pastry over filling, roll once, fold sides in, then roll up. Place seam-side down on baking sheet. Repeat with remaining ingredients.

Brush top of pastries with melted butter and bake until puffed and golden, about 25–30 minutes. Serve immediately.

NOTE: Commercial puff pastry may be used instead of filo: 12 oz (375 g) is sufficient. Roll out thinly, and cut into 4 rectangles about 6 x 8 in (15 x 20 cm) in size. Moisten sides and press to seal, instead of folding sides over filling. Bake in a preheated oven at 450°F (230°C/Gas 8) for 10 minutes, then reduce to 350°F (180°C/Gas 4) and cook for a further 15 minutes.

Braised lamb Taş kebapı

Serves 6
Cooking time 2 hours

2 lb (1 kg) boneless lamb stew meat
¼ cup (2 oz/60 g) butter
2 medium-sized onions, finely chopped
¼ cup (1½ oz/45 g) chopped green bell pepper
  (capsicum) (optional)
1½ cups (9 oz/280 g) chopped, peeled
  tomatoes or ¼ cup (2 oz/60 g) tomato paste
1–1½ cups (8–12 fl oz/250–375 ml) water
½ teaspoon ground allspice
salt and freshly ground black pepper
¼ cup (⅓ oz/10 g) chopped fresh flat-leaf
  (Italian) parsley
Sultan's Delight (Hünkâr Beğendi) (page 40) or
  White Pilaf (Beyaz Pilavı) (page 52) for
  serving

Trim meat and cut into ¾-in (2-cm) cubes.

Heat half of butter in a heavy-based saucepan, add meat and cook quickly to brown on all sides. Transfer to a plate as it browns and set aside.

Heat remaining butter in pan, and add onion and bell pepper if using. Cook gently until onion is translucent.

Add tomatoes or tomato paste and 1 cup (8 fl oz/250 ml) water if using tomatoes, more if using paste. Stir well to lift browned juices and add allspice, salt and pepper to taste, and most of parsley.

Return lamb to pan, cover and simmer gently until lamb is tender and sauce thickened, about 1½ hours.

Pile in center of Sultan's Delight. If serving with White Pilaf, press cooked pilav into an oiled ring mold and unmold onto a serving platter. Spoon some of sauce over rice and place meat in center.

Sprinkle meat with reserved chopped parsley and serve hot.

Lamb pie Mantı

Serves 4–5
Cooking time 1 hour

For pie crust:
2 cups (10 oz/300 g) all-purpose (plain) flour
½ teaspoon salt
¼ cup (2 fl oz/60 ml) oil
½ cup (4 fl oz/125 ml) cold water

For filling:
1 lb (500 g) finely ground (minced) lamb
1 tablespoon oil
1 small onion, finely chopped
2 tablespoons finely chopped fresh flat-leaf
  (Italian) parsley
salt
freshly ground black pepper

melted butter
1 cup (8 fl oz/250 ml) hot chicken stock
yogurt for serving

To make pie crust: Sift flour and salt into a mixing bowl. Add oil and rub into flour with fingertips. Add water, mix to a soft dough and knead lightly until smooth. Cover and let rest for 30 minutes.

To make filling: Place ground lamb in a mixing bowl; it should not be too lean. Heat oil in a frying pan, add onion and cook gently until translucent. Add to lamb with parsley and salt and pepper to taste, and mix to combine.

Roll out one-third of pie crust to fit a 10- x 12-in (25- x 30-cm) baking dish. Cover with a kitchen towel and set aside.

Roll out remaining pie crust thinly and cut into 1½-in(4-cm) squares. Place about 1 teaspoon meat filling in center of each square, fold up sides and press to seal. Finished parcels should look like miniature canoes with the meat filling showing.

Preheat oven to 350°F (180°C/Gas 4). Grease or butter a baking dish. Arrange finished parcels side by side in rows in baking dish. Cover with reserved pie crust, tucking edges in neatly. Brush top with melted butter.

Bake for 45 minutes. Remove from oven and pour hot chicken stock over pie crust. Return to oven and bake until most of stock is absorbed, a further 10–15 minutes.

Cut into squares and serve with yogurt.

NOTE: Sometimes this dish is prepared without the top covering of pastry, a more attractive way to present the dish. Brush the meat filling with butter before baking.

Lamb dumplings in yogurt Kurumantı

Serves 6
Cooking time 40 minutes

For dough:
2 cups (10 oz/300 g) all-purpose (plain) flour
½ teaspoon salt
1 egg
cold water

For filling:
6 oz (375 g) finely ground (minced) lamb
1 small onion, grated
2 tablespoons finely chopped fresh flat-leaf
  (Italian) parsley
salt
freshly ground black pepper

8 cups (64 fl oz/2 L) water
1 tablespoon salt
1 cup (8 fl oz/250 ml) strong chicken stock
2 cups (16 fl oz/500 ml) Drained Yogurt
  (page 125)
2 cloves garlic, crushed
2 teaspoons dried mint
fresh mint leaves for garnish

To make dough: Sift flour and salt into a mixing bowl. Beat egg with fork in a cup measure and make up to ½ cup (4 fl oz/ 125 ml) with cold water. Pour into flour and mix to a firm dough. Add a little more water if necessary. Knead until smooth, cover and let rest for 20–30 minutes.

To make filling: Combine all ingredients well, adding salt and pepper to taste.

To make dumplings: On a floured board or work surface, roll out half of dough as thinly as possible. Cut into 1½-in (4-cm) squares, stack and cover. Repeat with remaining half of dough.

Place 1 teaspoon meat filling in center of a square, moisten edges with water and fold over into a triangle, enclosing filling. Press edges well to seal. Bring two narrow angles of triangle together and press well, making a shape somewhat resembling the Italian tortellini. Place on a tray lined with kitchen towel and cover while making remainder.

Bring water to a boil in a large saucepan and add salt. Working in batches, add about 20 dumplings to pan, return to a boil and boil for 5 minutes. Remove using a slotted spoon to a colander to drain. Repeat to cook remaining dumplings. Cooked dumplings may be stored in a sealed container in the refrigerator if not required immediately.

When ready to serve, bring chicken stock to a boil in a large saucepan, add dumplings and boil gently for 5 minutes. Add yogurt and crushed garlic, and heat gently, stirring, for 2–3 minutes; do not allow sauce to boil. Rub mint to a powder and stir into sauce. Serve immediately, sprinkled with torn fresh mint leaves.

Wedding meat Düğün eti

Another wedding feast dish. Ingredient quantities have been scaled down considerably—even the Turks don't wait for a wedding just to prepare this spicy lamb dish.

Serves 6
Cooking time 2 hours

6 lamb shoulder chops, cut 1½ in (4 cm) thick
¼ cup (2 oz/60 g) butter
2 medium-sized onions, chopped
1½ cups (9 oz/280 g) chopped, peeled
  tomatoes
1 cup (8 fl oz/250 ml) water
1½ teaspoons ground cinnamon
½ teaspoon whole allspice, crushed
3 cloves
salt
freshly ground black pepper

For serving:
broiled (grilled) tomato slices
Wedding Pilaf (Düğün Pilavı) (page 52)

Trim chops if necessary. Heat half of butter in a heavy-based frying pan or large saucepan, add meat and cook until browned on each side. Remove and set aside on a plate.

Heat remaining butter in pan, add onions and cook gently until soft. Add tomatoes, water and spices, and stir well to lift browned juices. Bring to a boil, then reduce heat.

Return lamb to pan, and add salt and pepper to taste. Cover and simmer over low heat until meat is tender, 1½ hours. Remove cloves if desired.

Remove lamb from pan and arrange on a warm platter. Place broiled (grilled) tomato slices around lamb. Pour sauce over lamb. Serve with Wedding Pilaf.

Meatballs in tomato sauce
Izmir köftesi

Serves 5–6
Cooking time 1½ hours

1½ lb (750 g) finely ground (minced) beef or
   lamb
1 clove garlic, crushed
1 small onion, finely grated
2 thick slices stale white bread
cold water
1 egg
1 teaspoon ground cumin
2 tablespoons finely chopped fresh flat-leaf
   (Italian) parsley
salt
freshly ground black pepper
all-purpose (plain) flour for coating
¼ cup (2 oz/60 g) butter or ¼ cup
   (2 fl oz/60 ml) oil

For tomato sauce:
1½ cups (9 oz/280 g) chopped, peeled
   tomatoes
2 tablespoons tomato paste
½ cup (2½ oz/75 g) finely chopped green bell
   pepper (capsicum)
½ teaspoon sugar
salt
freshly ground black pepper
½ cup (4 fl oz/125 ml) water

White Pilaf (Beyaz Pilavı) (page 52) for serving

In a mixing bowl, combine meat with garlic and onion. Soak bread in cold water, squeeze dry and crumble into bowl. Add egg, cumin, parsley, and salt and pepper to taste. Blend thoroughly to a smooth paste.

With moistened hands, shape tablespoons of meat mixture into oval, sausage-like shapes. Coat lightly with flour.

Heat butter or oil in a large saucepan or deep frying pan with lid to fit, add meatballs and cook until lightly browned on all sides. Using a slotted spoon, remove to a plate.

To make tomato sauce: Add tomatoes, tomato paste and bell pepper to pan. Cook, stirring, over medium heat for 5 minutes. Add sugar, and salt and pepper to taste, then stir in water. Bring to a boil.

Return meatballs to pan with sauce. Bring to a slow simmer. Cover and simmer gently until meatballs are tender and sauce is thick, about 1 hour.

Serve with White Pilaf.

"Ladies' thighs" croquettes
Kadın budu

The Turks' appreciation of the fair sex is apparent even in the naming of recipes. Form the meat mixture with a certain voluptuousness to an elongated egg shape. Don't make them too plump—we all like to be flattered, don't we?

Serves 6
Cooking time about 20–25 minutes

1½ lb (750 g) finely ground (minced) lean lamb
　or beef
1 cup (5 oz/150 g) cooked rice
1 medium-sized onion, finely chopped
½ cup (2½ oz/75 g) crumbled beyaz peynir (feta
　cheese)
¼ cup (⅓ oz/10 g) finely chopped fresh parsley
1 teaspoon finely chopped fresh dill
salt
freshly ground black pepper
2 large eggs
oil for shallow-frying
½ cup (2½ oz/75 g) all-purpose (plain) flour for
　coating

In a large mixing bowl, combine meat, cooked rice, onion and cheese. Put mixture through meat grinder using fine screen.

Add herbs, salt and pepper to taste, and 1 lightly beaten egg. Mix by hand to a smooth paste.

Take 1 heaping tablespoon of mixture and form into an elongated egg shape, wider at one end than the other, or into simpler torpedo shape. Moisten hands with water to facilitate handling. Place croquettes side by side in a baking dish as they are finished.

Beat remaining egg well and pour over croquettes, then turn them over in dish to coat them evenly with a film of egg.

Heat oil in a frying pan. Place flour on a plate. Roll croquettes in flour, one at a time, and place into pan as they are coated. Use one hand for rolling them in flour, and keep other hand dry for placing them in pan.

Cook croquettes over high heat until golden-brown, turning frequently with tongs so that they hold their shape. Remove using a slotted spoon and drain on paper towels.

Serve hot with vegetable or salad accompaniment.

Fried meatballs Kuru köftesi

Serves 6
Cooking time 5–6 minutes per batch

1½ lb (750 g) finely ground (minced) lamb or
   beef
1 onion, roughly chopped
3 tablespoons chopped fresh flat-leaf (Italian)
   parsley
4–5 slices (about 3 oz/90 g) stale white bread,
   crusts removed
2 eggs
¼ teaspoon cayenne pepper
½ teaspoon paprika
½ teaspoon ground cumin
½ teaspoon ground allspice
1 teaspoon salt
½ teaspoon freshly ground black pepper

½ cup (2½ oz/75 g) all-purpose (plain) flour for
   coating
oil for shallow-frying
plain (natural) yogurt for serving
Spicy Pilaf (Iç Pilav) for serving (page 48)
   (optional)
salad vegetables for serving

Place ground lamb or beef in a large bowl and set aside.

Combine onion and parsley in a food processor and process until finely chopped. Soak bread in water and squeeze dry. Add bread to onion mixture with eggs, cayenne pepper, paprika, cumin, allspice, salt and black pepper. Process to a thick puree. Add puree to meat in bowl and mix through using a wooden spoon, then use hands to mix thoroughly. Cover and let stand for 10 minutes.

With moistened hands, shape mixture into balls the size of a large walnut and place on a tray. Sift flour into a deep dish.

Heat a large frying pan over medium heat. When hot, add oil to a depth of ¼ in (5 mm). Working with half of meatballs, coat in flour then add to hot oil and shallow-fry until browned all over, shaking pan and turning meatballs frequently to brown evenly, about 5–6 minutes. Remove using a slotted spoon and drain on paper towels. Repeat with remaining meatballs.

Serve hot or warm with yogurt, Spicy Pilaf, if desired, and salad vegetables.

NOTE: Lamb is the traditional meat used in Turkey for this recipe, but beef may be substituted if desired.

Lamb sausages with potatoes
Salçali köfte

Serves 4–6
Cooking time 1¼ hours

1½ lb (750 g) finely ground (minced) lamb
3 slices stale white bread, crusts removed
2 cloves garlic, crushed
2 tablespoons chopped fresh flat-leaf (Italian)
  parsley
1 teaspoon ground cumin
¼ teaspoon ground cinnamon
¼ teaspoon ground allspice
1 teaspoon salt
freshly ground black pepper

For tomato sauce:
⅓ cup (3 oz/90 g) tomato paste
½ small green bell pepper (capsicum), chopped
1 cup (8 fl oz/250 ml) water
½ teaspoon sugar
salt and freshly ground black pepper

6 medium potatoes
¼ cup (2 oz/60 g) butter, melted

Put lamb into a large mixing bowl. Soak bread in cold water and squeeze dry. Crumble onto lamb and add garlic, parsley, cumin, cinnamon, allspice, salt and plenty of pepper. Mix to combine, then knead vigorously with hand until paste-like in consistency, about 5 minutes. Alternatively, process mixture in 2 batches in a food processor for 3 minutes, then knead briefly to combine.

With moistened hands, shape heaping tablespoons of lamb mixture into oval, sausagelike rolls, placing them on a tray as they are shaped.

Preheat oven to 350°F (180°C/Gas 4).

To make tomato sauce: In a bowl, mix tomato paste with bell pepper, water, sugar, and salt and pepper to taste.

Peel and cut potatoes in half so that they are somewhat similar in shape to köfte. Brush a large baking dish with butter and arrange köfte and potatoes in alternate rows, placing potatoes cut-side down. Brush potatoes and köfte with remaining butter then pour tomato sauce over evenly.

Bake for 15 minutes, basting once with sauce in baking dish. Cover with aluminum foil and reduce oven temperature to 325°F (170°C/Gas 3). Cook until potatoes are tender, a further 1 hour. Check halfway through cooking and add a little more water to dish if necessary.

Serve hot with vegetables or a green salad.

Vegetables with lamb stuffing
Sebze dolması

Serves 6 as a main course, more for
a buffet
Cooking time 1½ hours

6 medium-sized green bell peppers (capsicums)
6 medium-sized tomatoes
6 long (Japanese) eggplants (aubergines)

For stuffing:
1½ lb (750 g) finely ground (minced) lamb
1 small onion, finely chopped
1 cup (6 oz/185 g) chopped, peeled tomatoes
¼ cup (2 oz/60 g) tomato paste
¼ cup (1½ oz/45 g) finely chopped green bell
  pepper (capsicum)
¼ cup (1½ oz/45 g) short-grain rice
½ cup (3 oz/90 g) coarse bulgur (burghul),
  rinsed
pinch cayenne pepper
1½ teaspoons salt

2 cups (16 fl oz/500 ml) water
3 tablespoons sumak
1 tablespoon tomato paste
1½ teaspoons salt
1 teaspoon sugar

Wash vegetables. Cut tops off peppers and reserve. Remove core, seeds and white membrane, rinse and drain. Cut tops (stem end) off tomatoes and reserve. Scoop out tomato pulp with a spoon and reserve pulp separately. Drain tomatoes. Remove stalks from eggplant. Cut off ¾ in (2 cm) from stalk end and reserve. Scoop out eggplant flesh, leaving ¼ in (5 mm) wall of flesh. Place eggplants in salted water and let soak for 20 minutes. Rinse and drain.

To make stuffing: Combine ingredients in a large mixing bowl and mix well.

Fill vegetables with stuffing; do not fill completely as there must be space for expansion. Replace all reserved tops. For eggplants, pare down reserved tops to form a cork.

Combine water and sumak in a saucepan, bring to a boil, then strain through a fine sieve into a bowl. Discard sumak, and add water if necessary to make liquid up to 2 cups (16 fl oz/500 ml).

Place reserved pulp from tomatoes in base of a large, deep, heavy-based saucepan. Arrange stuffed peppers upright in pan on top of tomato pulp. Arrange eggplants on top of peppers, placing them on their sides. Top with tomatoes, placed upright on eggplants.

Blend sumak liquid with tomato paste, salt and sugar, and pour evenly over vegetables. Cover pan tightly and bring to a boil. Reduce heat to low and simmer gently for 1¼ hours.

Carefully remove vegetables from pan, arrange in a serving dish and keep warm. Boil liquid in pan to reduce a little, then pour over vegetables. Serve hot or warm.

Skewered lamb and vegetables
Şiş kebapı

Serves 6
Cooking time 10–12 minutes

2 lb (1 kg) boneless lamb from leg
juice of 1 large lemon
¼ cup (2 fl oz/60 ml) olive oil
1 onion, thinly sliced
freshly ground black pepper
1 bay leaf, crumbled
½ teaspoon dried thyme

12 small whole onions
boiling salted water
1 red bell pepper (capsicum)
1 green bell pepper (capsicum)
salt

White Pilaf (Beyaz Pilavı) (page 52)

Cut lamb into 1¼-in (3-cm) cubes and place in a glass or ceramic bowl. Add lemon juice, olive oil, onion slices, pepper, bay leaf and thyme. Salt should not be added until after cooking as it tends to draw out meat juices. Cover and marinate in refrigerator for 4–6 hours, turning meat occasionally. Leave for longer if desired.

Peel whole onions and parboil in salted water for 5 minutes. Drain.

Wash bell peppers and remove core, seeds and white membrane. Cut into 1¼-in (3-cm) squares.

Remove lamb from marinade and thread onto 6 long skewers, alternating cubes of meat with whole onions and bell pepper pieces.

Cook over glowing charcoal for 10–12 minutes, turning frequently and brushing with marinade as required. After sealing meat, remove skewers to cooler part of grill or raise the grid, otherwise vegetables will burn.

Serve hot on a bed of White Pilaf.

NOTE: If desired, White Pilaf may be colored with ½ teaspoon turmeric, added to recipe when cooking rice in butter (see page 52).

Almond custard Keskül

Serves 6
Cooking time 45 minutes

¾ cup (3 oz/90 g) whole blanched almonds
4 cups (32 fl oz/1 L) cold milk
¼ cup (1 oz/30 g) ground rice
¼ teaspoon salt
¼ cup (2 oz/60 g) sugar
4 drops almond extract (essence)
chopped pistachio nuts or toasted slivered
   almonds for garnish
pomegranate seeds for garnish (optional)

Grind almonds finely in a food processor or blender, or pass through a food grinder 2 or 3 times using fine screen. Place in a mixing bowl and knead with your hand to a firm paste.

Heat 1 cup (8 fl oz/250 ml) cold milk to boiling point, pour onto almonds and stir with wooden spoon until well blended. Set aside to steep.

In a large mixing bowl, blend ¼ cup (2 fl oz/60 ml) cold milk with ground rice. In a heavy-based saucepan, preferably nonstick, heat remaining milk. Bring to a boil and pour onto ground rice mixture, stirring constantly, then return mixture to pan. Bring to a boil, add salt and simmer gently for 10 minutes, stirring occasionally.

Strain almond milk through a fine sieve into a bowl, pressing almonds with back of spoon. Pour almond milk into pan, stir well to combine, and stir in sugar. Simmer gently for a further 10 minutes.

Stir in almond extract and pour into individual dessert bowls. Serve garnished with chopped pistachio nuts or almonds and pomegranate seeds if using.

Ladies' navels Kadın göbeği

The name and the finished dish are colorfully Turkish, while the basic dough is very definitely French. Though the ingredient proportions differ from the traditional formula, it is choux nonetheless, prepared in the Turkish manner.

Makes about 20
Cooking time 40 minutes

For syrup:
1 cup (8 oz/250 g) sugar
1½ cups (12 fl oz/375 ml) water
strained juice of ½ lemon

For choux pastry:
1 cup (5 oz/150 g) all-purpose (plain) flour
¼ teaspoon salt
1 cup (8 fl oz/250 ml) water
¼ cup (2 oz/60 g) butter
2 large eggs, lightly beaten
⅛ teaspoon almond extract (essence)

oil for shaping and frying
whipped cream or Clotted Cream (Kaymak)
  (page 99) for serving
¼ cup (1 oz/30 g) finely chopped, blanched
  pistachio nuts for serving

To make syrup: In a heavy-based saucepan, dissolve sugar in water over medium heat, stirring occasionally. Bring to a boil, add lemon juice and boil rapidly, without stirring, for 15 minutes. Remove pan from heat and let syrup cool in pan.

To make choux pastry: Sift flour and salt onto a square of stiff paper. In another heavy-based saucepan, bring water and butter to a boil. Add flour all at once, stirring constantly with a wooden spoon or balloon whisk. Continue stirring until mixture pulls away from side of pan, then cook over low heat, stirring occasionally, for a further 5 minutes.

Transfer choux to a bowl and let cool for 2 minutes. Gradually beat in eggs. Add almond extract and beat until smooth and satiny. A balloon whisk will break up lumps, but a wooden spoon is better for a smooth finish, so utilize both for this step.

Oil hands. Take a walnut-sized portion of dough, roll into a smooth ball and place on an oiled tray. Flatten ball into a round about 2 in (5 cm) in diameter and press oiled forefinger into center to make a hole. Repeat with remaining dough. Keep hands oiled for shaping so dough will not stick.

To cook göbeği, add oil to a depth of ½ in (12 mm) in a large electric frying pan and heat until just warm. Add half of göbeği, immediately increase heat to 400°F (200°C) and cook until göbeği rise to surface and are puffed, then turn over. Continue to turn frequently during end of cooking time to brown göbeği evenly. This should take about 15 minutes in total, from when göbeği are first added to pan.

When cooked, remove from oil using a slotted spoon and let drain briefly on paper towels. (Turn off frying pan and let oil cool before cooking second batch.) Place göbeği into syrup, turn to coat, and let stand for 5 minutes. Remove to a plate.

To serve, arrange on a flat platter and place a dollop of cream in the center. Sprinkle with pistachio nuts.

NOTE: In place of an electric frying pan, use a large frying pan set on a thermostatically controlled hot plate or burner. Otherwise use an ordinary burner, heat oil at low and increase heat to medium–high when göbeği are added.

Lips of the beauty
Dilber dudağı

Follow recipe for Ladies' Navels (Kadın Göbeği) (page 98), except that these are shaped differently, as their name suggests. Flatten each ball of dough in your hands to form 2½-in (6-cm) rounds and fold over each round so that the curved side resembles lips. Place on an oiled tray as they are shaped. Cook and finish as for Ladies' Navels. Serve plain or with whipped cream or Clotted Cream (Kaymak) (page 99).

Dainty fingers
Hanım parmağı

Follow recipe for Ladies' Navels (Kadın Göbeği) (page 98) but do not form dough into balls. Instead take about 2 teaspoons dough and form into finger-like shapes about 3 in (8 cm) long. Place on an oiled tray. Keep hands oiled for shaping.

To cook, heat oil for deep-frying to 400°F (200°C) and deep-fry 8–10 at a time, turning to brown evenly, for 10 minutes. Drain briefly on paper towels then place into prepared syrup. Let soak in syrup for 5 minutes, then lift out and serve warm, piled on a platter. Sprinkle with finely chopped walnuts or pistachio nuts if desired.

Clotted cream
Kaymak

Traditionally in Turkey, kaymak is made of rich buffalo's milk which is boiled and left to stand until the cream forms solidly on top. It is so thick it can be cut with a knife. The cream is enjoyed with certain pastries or on its own with sweet preserves or honey. It does not melt on heating. As the flavor of the genuine kaymak is rather strong, it is an acquired taste. This version uses powdered cow's milk so the flavor, though different, is more widely acceptable. If you have access to rich milk fresh from the cow, it is possible to make clotted cream—in other words Devonshire cream is a good substitute where this is available.

Makes about 1 cup (8 fl oz/250 ml)
Cooking time 3 hours

2 cups (7 oz/220 g) full-cream powdered milk
2½ cups (20 fl oz/625 ml) water

Blend powdered milk with water thoroughly, beating if necessary to break up lumps.

Pour into a 9-in (23-cm) frying pan, preferably with a heavy base and also nonstick (which prevents milk from scorching). Bring slowly to a gentle simmer over medium–low heat; do not allow milk to boil.

When a cream skin forms on top, pull this to one side of pan with a large spoon. Lift out, pouring any liquid in spoon back into saucepan. Place cream in a bowl.

Each 10 minutes or so for the following 2–2½ hours, remove cream skin as it forms. At end, only a thin layer of thick milk remains in pan: this may be discarded or used in cooking.

Place collected cream in a blender or food processor and process until smooth. Pour back into bowl and refrigerate to chill thoroughly. Cream sets solidly and, if kept covered, will keep in the refrigerator for 1 week or more. Use as directed in recipes or with stewed fruits and desserts.

Poached apricots with cream
Kaymaklı kayısı tatlısı

You need soft Turkish apricots for this dessert, pitted but left whole—not dried in halves. In Turkey, these would be filled with Clotted Cream (Kaymak) (page 99).

Serves 4–6
Cooking time 25 minutes

6 oz (185 g) dried whole apricots
1½ cups (12 fl oz/375 ml) water
thinly peeled strip of lemon zest
½ cup (4 oz/125 g) sugar
1 teaspoon lemon juice
¾ cup (6 fl oz/180 ml) Clotted Cream (Kaymak)
   (page 99) or extra heavy (double) cream or
   crème fraîche
2 tablespoons finely chopped, blanched
   pistachio nuts for serving

Rinse apricots and place in a saucepan with water and lemon zest. Cover, slowly bring to a gentle boil then boil for 10 minutes until soft. Add sugar and lemon juice, and shake pan gently until sugar is dissolved; avoid stirring or apricots could break up. Bring to a boil, cover and simmer over low heat for 10 minutes. Remove pan from heat and let cool to lukewarm.

Using a slotted spoon, transfer apricots to a sieve, allowing excess syrup to drain back into pan, then set aside. Return syrup to a boil and boil for 1 minute. Strain syrup through fine sieve into a pitcher. Let cool and refrigerate until chilled.

Meanwhile, gently open each apricot and insert 1 heaping teaspoon clotted cream. Close apricot partially; cream should be visible. Arrange in serving dish in a single layer. Cover and refrigerate until required. To serve, pour cooled syrup around apricots and sprinkle with pistachios.

Yogurt cake Yogurt tatlısı

Serves 8–10
Cooking time 50–55 minutes

¾ cup (6 oz/185 g) butter
grated zest of 1 lemon
1 cup (7 oz/220 g) superfine (caster) sugar
5 eggs, separated
1 cup (8 fl oz/250 ml) plain (natural) yogurt
2¼ cups (11 oz/330 g) all-purpose (plain) flour
2 teaspoons baking powder
pinch salt
½ teaspoon baking soda (bicarbonate of soda)

For syrup:
1 cup (8 oz/250 g) sugar
¾ cup (6 fl oz/180 ml) cold water
thin strip lemon zest
1 tablespoon strained lemon juice

Preheat oven to 350°F (180°C/Gas 4). Grease and lightly flour an 8-in (20-cm) tube cake pan.

In a mixing bowl, cream butter, lemon zest and sugar until light and fluffy. Add egg yolks one at a time, beating well after each addition. Add yogurt and mix to combine.

Sift flour, baking powder, salt and baking soda into a separate bowl. Fold into butter mixture.

In a clean bowl, beat egg whites until stiff and then fold into cake batter. Pour batter into prepared cake pan. Bake for 50–55 minutes; when cooked, a fine skewer inserted into center of cake should come out clean.

Meanwhile, make syrup: Combine sugar and water in a saucepan over medium heat, stirring until dissolved. Bring to a boil, add lemon zest and juice, and boil, over medium heat, without stirring, for 10 minutes. Remove pan from heat, discard lemon zest, and let syrup cool.

Let cake cool in pan for 5 minutes, then turn out onto a serving dish. Spoon cold syrup over cake, letting it seep slowly into cake. Serve warm, cut in thick slices with whipped cream or Clotted Cream (Kaymak) (page 99).

Semolina halva with saffron and pistachios Irmik helvası

Halva is Turkey's oldest sweet, and can be made with flour, nuts and grape syrup, or with semolina. Do not confuse this halva with the sesame seed confection of the same name. The saffron in this recipe does not become a powder, but the flavor is released more readily when pounded in a mortar. Take care when adding the milk syrup to the semolina as it may spatter a little.

Serves 6–8
Cooking time 35 minutes

¼ **teaspoon saffron threads**
1 **tablespoon hot water**
3 **cups (24 fl oz/750 ml) milk**
¾ **cup (6 oz/185 g) sugar**
⅓ **cup (3 oz/90 g) unsalted butter**
⅓ **cup (1½ oz/45 g) pistachio nuts**
¾ **cup (4 oz/125 g) coarse semolina**

Pound saffron strands in a mortar using a pestle, add hot water and let stand for 10 minutes.

Heat milk in a saucepan. Add sugar and stir until dissolved. Stir in saffron water and bring slowly to a gentle boil.

Meanwhile, melt about 1 teaspoon butter in a heavy-based saucepan over medium heat. Add pistachio nuts and cook 2–3 minutes; do not brown. Remove and set aside.

Place remaining butter and semolina in saucepan over medium–low heat and cook, stirring often, for 10 minutes; do not allow to color. Remove pan from heat and stir in boiling milk syrup. Return to heat and stir constantly until thickened and beginning to bubble. Boil gently for 2 minutes, stir in nuts, and remove from heat. Transfer to bowl and serve warm or at room temperature.

Shredded pastries with pistachios
Burma kadayıf

Shredded pastry is usually sold under the Greek name kataifi at Middle Eastern markets. It is made with a thin dough poured through a perforated screen onto a hotplate, dried briefly, then the strands are scooped off. A bamboo sushi mat can be used to assist in rolling the pastries.

Makes 20
Cooking time about 1 hour

12 oz (375 g) kataifi pastry
¾ cup (6 fl oz/185 ml) melted unsalted butter

For syrup:
1 cup (8 fl oz/250 ml) water
1½ cups (12 oz/375 g) sugar
1 teaspoon strained lemon juice
3 teaspoons rose water or orange flower water

For pistachio filling:
1 egg white
¼ cup (2 oz/60 g) superfine (caster) sugar
1½ cups (6 oz/185 g) chopped pistachio nuts
1 cup (5 oz/150 g) chopped blanched almonds
1 teaspoon rose water or orange flower water

3 tablespoons finely chopped, blanched
  pistachio nuts for serving

Remove package of pastry from refrigerator 2 hours before required to bring it to room temperature. Melt butter and place in bowl in pan of hot water to keep warm.

To make syrup: Place water, sugar and lemon juice in a heavy-based saucepan over medium heat and stir until sugar is dissolved. Bring to a boil and boil for 12 minutes. Add rose water or orange flower water, stir and remove pan from heat. Let cool completely.

Preheat oven to 325°F (170°C/Gas 3). Grease a 7- x 11-in (18- x 28-cm) shallow cake pan or baking dish with butter.

To make filling: Beat egg white in a bowl until stiff. Gradually beat in sugar. Fold in nuts and rose water or orange flower water.

To assemble: With kataifi still in package, squeeze and knead to loosen strands. Take one-fourth of kataifi and spread on a board, roughly with strands running away from you. Shape into a 7- x 11-in (18- x 28-cm) rectangle, with short edge in front of you. Using a brush, dab strands with melted butter. Place about one-fourth of filling along lower edge and roll up firmly into neat roll. Repeat to make another 3 rolls.

Arrange rolls in prepared pan or dish, spacing a little apart. Brush remaining butter over rolls. Bake until golden and crisp, about 40 minutes.

Remove from oven and pour cold syrup evenly over hot rolls. Cover with folded white paper towels and let stand until syrup has been absorbed and rolls are cold. To serve, cut each roll crosswise into 5 pieces and sprinkle tops with chopped blanched pistachio nuts. Store in a sealed container at room temperature.

Turkish delight Lokum

Cooking time 1½ hours
Makes about 2 lb (1 kg)

4 cups (2 lb/1 kg) granulated sugar
4½ cups (36 fl oz/1.1 L) water
1 teaspoon lemon juice
1 cup (4 oz/125 g) cornstarch (cornflour)
1 teaspoon cream of tartar
1–2 tablespoons rose water
red food coloring
½ cup (2½ oz/75 g) chopped, toasted almonds,
    unblanched (optional)
¾ cup (3 oz/90 g) confectioners' (icing) sugar
additional ¼ cup (1 oz/30 g) cornstarch
    (cornflour)

Combine sugar, 1½ cups (12 fl oz/375 ml) water and lemon juice in a heavy-based saucepan over low heat. Stir until sugar dissolves, brushing sugar crystals off side of pan with a brush dipped in cold water.

Bring to a boil and boil to soft ball stage, 240°F (115°C) on a candy thermometer. Remove from heat.

In another heavy-based saucepan, blend cornstarch, cream of tartar and 1 cup (8 fl oz/250 ml) cold water until smooth. Boil remaining 2 cups (16 fl oz/500 ml) water and stir into cornstarch mixture. Place pan over medium heat and cook, stirring constantly, until mixture thickens and bubbles. Use a balloon whisk if lumps form.

Pour hot syrup gradually into pan, stirring constantly. Bring to a boil and boil gently, stirring occasionally with a wooden spoon, until mixture is a pale golden color, about 1¼ hours; stirring is essential.

Stir in rose water to taste and a few drops of red food coloring to get a pale pink color. Blend in nuts if using, and remove pan from heat.

Pour mixture into an oiled 9-in (23-cm) square cake pan and let stand for 12 hours to set.

Combine confectioners' sugar and extra ¼ cup (1 oz/30 g) cornflour in a flat dish.

Cut Turkish delight into squares with an oiled knife and toss squares in sugar mixture. Store in a sealed container with remaining sugar mixture sprinkled between layers.

VARIATIONS

Crème de Menthe lokum
Replace rose water and red food coloring with 2 tablespoons Crème de Menthe liqueur and a little green food coloring. Omit nuts.

Orange lokum
Use 1–2 tablespoons orange flower water instead of rose water; use orange food coloring.

Vanilla lokum
Use 2 teaspoons vanilla extract (essence) instead of rose water and coloring, and use almonds or walnuts.

Bird's nest pastries Kusyuvası

Makes 20
Cooking time 35 minutes

For syrup:
2½ cups (1¼ lb/625 g) sugar
1½ cups (12 fl oz/375 ml) water
thinly peeled zest of ½ lemon
strained juice of 1½ lemons

For nut filling:
1½ cups (6 oz/185 g) finely chopped, blanched
   almonds
½ cup (2 oz/60 g) finely chopped, blanched
   pistachio nuts
2 tablespoons superfine (caster) sugar

20 sheets Yufka (Filo Pastry) (pages 28–9)
¾ cup (6 fl oz/180 ml) melted, unsalted butter

In a heavy-based saucepan over medium heat, combine sugar and water, stirring occasionally, until sugar dissolves. Bring to a boil, add lemon zest and juice and boil, without stirring, for 15 minutes. Remove from heat, let cool and strain into a pitcher. Refrigerate until required.

To make filling: Combine almonds and pistachios, reserving one-third of mixture. Stir sugar into remaining two-thirds.

Open out filo sheets and place between 2 dry kitchen towels. Cover top with a lightly dampened kitchen towel to prevent pastry drying out. Take 1 filo sheet and spread out on work surface. Brush with melted butter and fold in half lengthwise to make almost a square. Brush again with butter and sprinkle 1 tablespoon nut filling near folded edge. Turn pastry over filling, fold in ½ in (12 mm) on each side, and roll up to within 1½ in (4 cm) of other edge.

Lift up pastry by rolled edge with the flap hanging towards you and twirl into a ring, curling it away from you. Tuck loose pastry under, into center of ring, to form a nest. Repeat with remaining ingredients.

Place pastries in a greased baking dish and brush tops lightly with butter. Bake in a preheated oven at 350°F (180°C/Gas 4) until golden, 20–25 minutes.

Remove baking dish from oven and pour half of cold syrup over hot pastries. Let stand until cool, then sprinkle some reserved nuts into center of each pastry. Transfer pastries to serving platter and serve remaining syrup in a pitcher for adding to individual taste.

NOTE: For a special dessert, pile fresh strawberries in center of each cooled pastry and then sprinkle with nuts.

Baklava Baklava

Makes 30 pieces
Cooking time 1 hour

20 sheets Yufka (Filo Pastry) (pages 28–9)
¾ cup (6 fl oz/180 ml) melted, unsalted butter
2 cups (10 oz/300 g) finely chopped almonds
1 cup (4 oz/125 g) finely chopped walnuts
½ cup (3½ oz/110 g) superfine (caster) sugar
1 teaspoon ground cinnamon
⅛ teaspoon ground cloves

For syrup:
1½ cups (12 oz/375 g) sugar
1½ cups (12 fl oz/375 ml) water
¼ cup (3 oz/90 g) honey
thinly peeled strip of lemon zest
small piece cinnamon stick
3 cloves
2 teaspoons lemon juice

Preheat oven to 325°F (170°C/Gas 3). Butter base and sides of a 13- x 9- x 2-in (33- x 23- x 5-cm) baking dish.

Place 1 sheet filo into dish, brush with melted butter, then place another sheet on top and brush with butter again. Repeat until there are 9 buttered sheets in dish.

Combine nuts, sugar, cinnamon and cloves, and spread half of mixture over filo. Cover with another 2 sheets of filo, brushing each with melted butter.

Spread remaining nuts on top and finish with remaining filo, brushing each sheet with melted butter as before.

Trim edges and brush top with melted butter. Using a sharp knife, cut into diamond shapes (see page 29). Sprinkle lightly with water to prevent top layers from curling upwards during cooking.

Place on center shelf in preheated oven and bake for 30 minutes. Then move up one shelf and bake for further 30 minutes.

Cover with greased brown paper or aluminum foil if top colors too quickly. Pastry must be allowed to cook thoroughly.

Meanwhile, make syrup: Place sugar, water and honey in a heavy-based saucepan over medium heat and stir until sugar is dissolved. Add remaining syrup ingredients, bring to a boil and boil for 15 minutes. Strain syrup into a pitcher and let cool.

Pour cooled syrup evenly over hot baklava. Let stand for several hours before cutting into serving portions.

Figs in syrup Incir kompostu

Serves 6–8
Cooking time 45 minutes

3 cups (1 lb/500 g) dried figs
4 cups (32 fl oz/1 L) cold water
blanched almonds
¾ cup (6 oz/185 g) sugar
thin strip lemon zest
juice of 1 lemon
¼ cup (3 oz/90 g) honey

For serving:
chopped almonds, pistachios or walnuts
whipped cream or yogurt

Wash figs well and cover with cold water. Let stand until plump, about 8 hours. Drain water into a heavy-based saucepan and reserve.

Insert 1 almond into each fig, pushing almond in through base. Set aside.

Add sugar to reserved soaking water in saucepan and heat, stirring occasionally, until sugar is dissolved. Add lemon zest, juice and honey, and bring to a boil.

Add prepared figs and return to a boil. Boil gently, uncovered, until figs are tender and syrup is thick, about 30 minutes. Remove lemon zest.

Transfer figs to a bowl, arranging them upright. Pour syrup over figs, let cool, cover and refrigerate.

Sprinkle with chopped nuts and serve with whipped cream or yogurt.

Dried fruit compote Hoşafı

Serves 6
Cooking time 45 minutes

1 cup (6 oz/185 g) pitted prunes
1 cup (6 oz/185 g) dried apricot halves
1 cup (6 oz/185 g) golden raisins (sultanas)
water
½ cup (4 oz/125 g) sugar
thin strip lemon zest
2 cloves
¼ teaspoon ground allspice (optional)
chopped walnuts for serving

Wash dried fruits well and place in a saucepan with enough cold water to cover. Bring to a boil, then simmer, covered, on low heat for 15 minutes.

Add sugar, lemon zest, cloves and allspice if using. Stir until sugar is dissolved, adding a little more water if necessary. Simmer gently, uncovered, until fruit is soft but not mushy, and syrup is thick. Remove lemon zest and cloves.

Transfer to a bowl and refrigerate well to chill. Serve in dessert glasses sprinkled with chopped walnuts.

Noah's pudding Aşure

The credit for this dish goes back a long, long way. Of course it is pure assumption, but it illustrates the romantic nature of the Turks. It is said that on the last day on the Ark, the women used up all the remaining foods and came up with Aşure.

In Turkey today this pudding is prepared with great ceremony during the month of Muharrem, also known as the month of Aşure. Usually a vast quantity is made so that some may be given to friends and relatives. It is considered impolite not to give any to any person who may catch the cooking aroma.

As the right wheat for Aşure is difficult to find outside of the Middle East, the recipe is usually made with coarse bulgur elsewhere.

Serves 12–16
Cooking time 4½ hours

½ cup (3 oz/90 g) chickpeas
½ cup (3½ oz/110 g) dried haricot (navy) beans
water
1 cup (6 oz/185 g) coarse bulgur (burghul)
½ cup (3½ oz/110 g) short-grain rice
1½ cups (12 oz/375 g) sugar
½ teaspoon salt
1½ cups (12 fl oz/375 ml) milk
½ cup (3 oz/90 g) golden raisins (sultanas)
¼ cup (1½ oz/45 g) currants
½ cup (3 oz/90 g) chopped dried apricots
½ cup (3 oz/90 g) chopped dried figs
½ cup (2½ oz/75 g) chopped blanched almonds
½ cup (2 oz/60 g) chopped walnuts
¼ cup (1½ oz/45 g) pine nuts
¼ cup (2 fl oz/60 ml) rose water
pomegranate seeds, almonds or pistachio nuts
　for garnish

Wash chickpeas and beans well, and place in separate bowls. Pour 1½ cups (12 fl oz/375 ml) cold water in each bowl and let stand overnight.

Rinse bulgur and rice, and place in separate bowls. Add 4 cups (32 fl oz/1 L) cold water to bulgur; 1 cup (8 fl oz/250 ml) water to rice. Let stand overnight.

When ready to use, put chickpeas and beans in separate saucepans with enough fresh water to cover and cook until tender, about 1½–2 hours each. Chickpeas will take longer to cook than beans.

Put bulgur with its soaking water and an additional 3 cups (24 fl oz/750 ml) water in a large heavy-based saucepan. Drain rice and add to pan with bulgur. Place pan over low heat and cook gently, uncovered, until very soft and porridge-like in consistency, 40–50 minutes.

Drain cooked chickpeas and beans and add to bulgur and rice. Stir in an additional 1 cup (8 fl oz/250 ml) water. Cook over low heat, uncovered and stirring occasionally, until liquid is well reduced and pudding is thick, a further 30 minutes.

Stir in sugar, salt and milk, and cook for a further 15 minutes. Stir in fruits and nuts, and remove pan from heat. Add rose water, and stir well. Pour into 1 large serving bowl or individual dessert bowls.

Let cool to room temperature and serve, or cover and refrigerate to chill before serving. Garnish pudding with pomegranate seeds if available, otherwise garnish with blanched almonds or pistachio nuts.

Sultan's turbans Sarığı burma

To make these delicate pastries, it is important to have very fresh, pliable yufka (filo pastry) sheets as the roll has to be crumpled up. Brittle pastry breaks. If you find early attempts fail, then shape remaining ingredients as directed at end of the method. For filo recipe and hints, see pages 28–9.

Makes 24
Cooking time 30 minutes

For syrup:
2 cups (1 lb/500 g) sugar
1½ cups (12 fl oz/375 ml) water
1 tablespoon lemon juice
small piece cinnamon stick
2 cloves

For nut filling:
2 cups (8 oz/250 g) finely ground almonds or
   walnuts
¼ cup (2 oz/60 g) superfine (caster) sugar
1 teaspoon ground cinnamon

24 sheets Yufka (Filo Pastry) (pages 28–9)
¾ cup (6 fl oz/180 ml) warm, melted, unsalted
   butter

In a heavy-based saucepan over medium heat, combine sugar and water, stirring occasionally, until sugar dissolves. Bring to a boil. Add lemon juice, cinnamon and cloves, and boil, without stirring, for 15 minutes. Skim if required. Remove from heat, strain and let cool.

To make nut filling: Combine all ingredients in a mixing bowl.

Preheat oven to 350°F (180°C/Gas 4). Butter a baking dish or pan. Have ready a length of wooden dowelling, about ¼ in (5 mm) in diameter and 20 in (50 cm) long. To keep butter warm, place in a bowl in a saucepan of hot water.

Take 1 sheet filo pastry and spread out on work surface with longer edge toward you. Brush lightly and evenly with warm melted butter. Sprinkle 2 tablespoons nut filling evenly across lower one-third of pastry, keeping 1¼ in (3 cm) clear of base and just a little in from sides. Fold bottom edge of pastry over filling and place wooden dowelling along edge. Roll pastry, with filling firmly over dowelling, to end of sheet. Make sure end of pastry sticks on firmly; if not, brush again with a little warm melted butter.

Grip dowelling at each end of pastry and push hands gradually toward one another, crumpling up pastry evenly as you push. When evenly crumpled and with pastry roll less than half its original length, slide roll off dowelling onto work surface. Trim ends of roll, then twist into a flat snail-like coil.

Repeat with remaining ingredients taking care that pastry does not dry out, otherwise shaping will be difficult.

Place completed pastries close together in a prepared baking dish or pan. Brush lightly with melted butter and bake until light golden-brown, about 25–30 minutes.

Remove from oven and pour cooled syrup over hot pastries. Let stand in dish until cold then serve or store in a sealed container at room temperature.

ALTERNATIVE SHAPING: Assemble and roll on dowel as above, then slide pastry off onto work surface. Cut roll with a sharp knife into 4-in (10-cm) lengths. Place pastries in buttered baking dish, and cook as above.

Strawberry water ice
Çilekli dondurma

Serves 6–8

For syrup:
2 cups (16 fl oz/500 ml) water
1 cup (8 oz/250 g) sugar
2 teaspoons lemon juice

2 cups (16 fl oz/500 ml) strawberry puree (see Note)
1 teaspoon strained lemon juice
¼ cup (2 fl oz/60 ml) milk
red food coloring

In a heavy-based saucepan over medium heat, combine water and sugar, and stir until sugar is dissolved. Add 2 teaspoons lemon juice and bring to a boil. Boil for 5 minutes, skimming when necessary. Remove from heat and let stand until cool.

Combine strawberry puree with cooled syrup, strained lemon juice and milk, and stir in a few drops of food coloring. Pour into a freezer tray or loaf cake pan and freeze.

Spoon into chilled dessert glasses and serve immediately. If desired, ice can be broken up with a fork before placing into glasses.

NOTE: To make strawberry puree, wash and drain strawberries, remove hulls, and push strawberries through a fine sieve. A heaping 3 cups (12 oz/375 g) strawberries should yield 2 cups (16 fl oz/500 ml) puree.

Lemon water ice
Limonlu dondurma

Serves 6–8

4 lemons
3 cups (24 fl oz/750 ml) water
1 cup (8 oz/250 g) sugar
1 egg white
lemon food coloring (optional)

Wash lemons well. Peel zest thinly from lemons so that there is little or no pith left on zest.

Put zest in a saucepan with water and bring slowly to a boil. Boil uncovered for 10 minutes. Strain into a measuring pitcher and discard zest. If necessary, add water to make up liquid to 2 cups (16 fl oz/500 ml) and return to pan.

Add sugar to pan and cook over medium heat, stirring occasionally, until dissolved. Bring to a boil and boil over medium heat for 5 minutes. Remove from heat and let stand to cool.

Juice lemons and strain juice. Measure ¾ cup (6 fl oz/180 ml) juice and add to cooled syrup. Pour into a bowl and place in freezer. When half frozen, stir well to break up ice crystals and return to freezer.

Beat egg white in a bowl until stiff. Blend well into half-frozen syrup with a little lemon food coloring if using. Return to freezer and freeze until just firm.

Remove from freezer and beat well until smooth and light. Pour into a loaf cake pan, cover with aluminum foil and freeze until very firm, about 3 hours or longer.

To serve, draw a metal spoon across ice and place flaky curls into chilled dessert glasses. Alternatively scoop out using an ice-cream scoop.

Orange water ice
Portakali dondurma

Serves 6–8

thinly peeled zest of 2 oranges
thinly peeled zest of 1 lemon
3 cups (24 fl oz/750 ml) water
1 cup (8 oz/250 g) sugar
1 cup (8 fl oz/250 ml) orange juice
¼ cup (2 fl oz/60 ml) lemon juice

Follow recipe as for Lemon Water Ice (page 116), boiling both orange and lemon zests in water to make syrup.

Juice oranges and lemon, and add juice to cooled syrup. Pour into a bowl and freeze until firm, about 3 hours. Flake with a fork, pile flakes into chilled dessert glasses and serve immediately.

NOTE: Orange food coloring may be added to syrup if desired.

Cherry water ice
Kırazli dondurma

Follow recipe ingredients and method as for Strawberry Water Ice (page 116), substituting 2 cups (16 fl oz/500 ml) cherry puree for strawberry puree. To make cherry puree, wash and pit about 3 cups (1 lb/500 g) cherries and puree in food processor or blender. Add red food coloring only if necessary. Freeze and serve in chilled dessert glasses.

preserves

Apricot jam Kayısı reçeli

Makes about 3 cups
Cooking time 50 minutes

2 cups (12 oz/375 g) dried apricots
3 cups (24 fl oz/750 ml) cold water
juice of 1 lemon
3 cups (1½ lb/750 g) sugar
½ cup (2½ oz/75 g) blanched, split almonds
  (optional)

Wash apricots very well in cold water. Cut into small pieces and place in a bowl with 3 cups (24 fl oz/750 ml) water. Let soak for 12 hours.

Put apricots and their soaking water in a preserving pan. Add lemon juice and bring to a boil. Boil gently, covered, until apricots are very soft, about 30 minutes.

Add sugar and stir to dissolve. Return to a boil and boil quickly, stirring often. Boil for 15 minutes then test a little on a cold saucer. Draw finger across surface of cooled jam; it is ready when surface wrinkles; make sure you remove jam from heat while testing. Return to heat if necessary and test again after 5 minutes.

Stir in almonds if using and pour jam into hot, sterilized jars. Seal jars while hot. Store in a cool place.

STERILIZING JARS

Preserves and jams should be packed into sterilized jars to ensure good keeping qualities. Wash jars well in hot soapy water, rinse and drain. Stand upright on a baking sheet and place in cold oven. Close door and set oven temperature to 275°F (140°C/Gas 1). Once this temperature is reached, turn off oven and leave jars in oven until required for filling. Boil lids in a saucepan of water to sterilize.

Strawberry jam
Çilekli reçeli

Makes about 4 cups
Cooking time 50 minutes

8 cups (2 lb/1 kg) strawberries
juice of 2 lemons
3½ cups (1¾ lb/875 g) sugar

Wash and hull strawberries. Cut strawberries in half and place in a preserving pan with lemon juice.

Set on medium heat, cover pan and bring to a boil. Reduce heat to low and simmer gently until fruit is very soft, 20–30 minutes.

Remove pan from heat and add sugar. Stir to combine, then return to medium heat, stirring again to dissolve sugar. Bring to a boil and boil over medium heat until jam sets when a little is tested on a cold saucer, about 15 minutes. See Apricot Jam recipe (page 118) for more detail on testing.

Let jam cool a little, then ladle into hot, sterilized jars (see page 118). Seal jars while hot. Store in a cool place.

Rose petal jam
Gül reçeli

Makes about 2 cups
Cooking time 25 minutes

4 cups (3½ oz/100 g) fragrant red rose petals
3 cups (1½ lb/750 g) sugar
2 cups (16 fl oz/500 ml) water
juice of ½ lemon

Snip off white base of each rose petal with kitchen scissors and discard. Wash petals gently in cold water and drain.

Layer petals in a bowl, sprinkling 2 tablespoons sugar on each layer. Let stand overnight.

Next day put remaining sugar and water in a heavy-based saucepan over medium heat. Stir occasionally until sugar is dissolved then bring to a boil. Add lemon juice and boil for a further 5 minutes without stirring. Remove pan from heat and let cool to lukewarm.

Stir rose petals and their liquid into syrup and return pan to heat. Bring slowly to a boil and boil gently until syrup is thick when tested on a cold saucer, about 15 minutes. See Apricot Jam recipe (page 118) for more detail on testing.

Ladle jam into hot, sterilized jars. Seal jars while hot. Store in a cool place.

beverages

Turkish coffee Kahve

The coffee is prepared in a small, long-handled pot tapering in at the top, called a "cezve." The purist (and they all are in Turkey when it comes to making coffee) would grind the beans to a fine powder just before brewing. Turkish brass coffee mills are sold throughout the Middle East.

When offered a cup, you will be asked if you like it sade (unsweetened), orta (moderately sweetened), or çok sekerli (very sweet).

Turkish coffee or "kahve" ideally is made one cup at a time, or three at the most. Place 1 demitasse cup cold water into jezve and add 1 heaping teaspoon powdered Turkish coffee and sugar if desired; 1 level teaspoon for orta, or 1 heaping teaspoon or more for çok sekerli. Stir and heat over medium–low heat. When coffee rises in pot, remove from pot from heat immediately, and spoon froth into cup.

Return pot to heat and cook until coffee rises again. Remove from heat and fill cup. Some prefer to heat coffee 3 times in all, though twice is sufficient, particularly if only making 1 cup. When using the repeated heating method, a little froth is spooned into each cup each time the pot is removed from the heat, as a good cup of kahve must have a creamy foam floating on top. Do not drink the grounds in the bottom of the cup.

appendix: nuts and yogurt

Nuts

ALMOND
Bot: *Prunus dulcis*
Turkish: badem
Purchase in shells or, for easier storage, already shelled but not blanched if they are to be stored for a while. The skin prevents the kernel drying and losing flavorsome oils. Store in a sealed container, in the refrigerator during summer when certain insects decide to multiply.
To blanch: Pour boiling water over kernels, let stand for 2–3 minutes and drain. When cool enough to handle, squeeze nut and kernel will pop out of skin.
To split almonds: Separate halves with a fine-bladed knife.

To sliver almonds: Let soak a little longer when blanching, to soften kernel, then cut into 3 or 4 slivers. If almonds are very crisp, slivers will break in the wrong places. Dry out slivers in oven at 250°F (130°C/Gas ½).
To chop: Use a nut chopper, food processor or blender, and chop to degree required.
To grind: Use a nut grinder or food processor. A blender is likely to cause oils to separate. Almonds should be dry and crisp for grinding finely.

WALNUT
Bot: *Juglans regia*
Turkish: ceviz
For peak flavor, purchase walnuts in shells, or buy ready-shelled from a reputable retailer. If walnut halves are required, it is best to purchase ready-shelled nuts, as any frustrated walnut cracker will confirm. Store, chop and grind as for almonds.

PISTACHIO NUT
Bot: *Pistacia vera*
Turkish: fıstık
Unsalted pistachio nuts are the ones required for cooking. Usually purchased in the shell. Break open and remove kernel. Store, blanch, chop and grind as for almonds.

HAZELNUT
Bot: *Corylus avellana*
Turkish: fındık
Buy ready-shelled. Blanch as for almonds and dry in oven at 250°F (130°C/Gas ½). Alternatively, place in a preheated oven at 350°F (180°C/Gas 4) for 10 minutes. Rub in a kitchen towel to remove skins. Store, chop and grind as for almonds.

CHESTNUTS

Bot: *Castanea sativa*

Turkish: kestane

Native to Mediterranean regions, chestnuts have been used from ancient times. To prepare for cooking, cut through shell at each end, cover with water and boil for 10 minutes. Remove a few at a time and peel off shell and inner covering on nut. To roast, cut a cross on one side of shell, place in a preheated oven at 350°F (180°C/Gas 4) and roast for 10–15 minutes. Peel while hot.

PINE NUTS

Bot: *Pinus pinea*

Turkish: çamfıstığı

Also called pignolia nuts, these are the kernels from the cones of the stone or umbrella pine, native to the Mediterranean region. Pine nuts are evenly oval and slender; there is another nut sometimes sold as pine nut, but it is tear-shaped and actually the pinon (pronounced pi'nyon) nut, from pines native to north-west America. Pinon nuts are less expensive.

Yogurt

Many Turkish dishes include, or are served, with homemade yogurt. Commercially made plain (natural) yogurt may be substituted, preferably a thick country-style or Greek-style variety.

Equipment required: 6-cup (48-fl oz/1.5-L) jar with lid; six sterilized 1-cup (8-fl oz/250-ml) jars or three 2-cup (16-fl oz/500-ml) jars (see page 118); preserving pan or large pot; thermometer; blanket or thick towels.

Mix ¾ cup (2½ oz/75 g) full-fat milk powder or skim milk powder into 6 cups (48 fl oz/1.5 L) whole milk, preferably homogenized. Pour into clean jar, cover with lid and stand in a pan of water. Heat water until milk temperature is 175°F (80°C). Remove jar from hot water and cool to 115°F (46°C). Remove ¼ cup (2 fl oz/60 ml) warm milk and blend with ¼ cup (2 fl oz/60 ml) starter (fresh, commercially made plain/natural yogurt). Stir into milk in jar, then pour into smaller jars. Seal jars with lids and stand in preserving pan. Add water to pan to come up to necks of jars. Heat until water temperature is 120°F (49°C) and remove from heat. Cover pan with lid, then wrap in thick towels or a blanket. Leave undisturbed for 3 hours. Remove jars, screw lids on tightly and store in refrigerator.

Yogurt made this way will keep in good condition for 7 to 10 days, with little change in the balance of the culture. Use some of this for your next yogurt. After making 3 or 4 batches, it is advisable to begin with a fresh starter.

A thermostatically controlled yogurt maker is a good investment for those who make yogurt frequently as it is so simple to use and ensures good results.

LOW-FAT YOGURT

Use skimmed milk and skim milk powder instead of whole milk and full-fat powdered milk.

DRAINED YOGURT

Recipes often call for drained yogurt. Simply place yogurt in a muslin (cheesecloth) or doubled piece of butter muslin, tie with string and suspend from a fixed object over a receptacle to collect draining liquid. Leave for 2–4 hours depending on initial thickness of yogurt. When drained, yogurt should have the consistency of softened cream cheese.

index

guide to weights and measures

The metric weights and metric fluid measures used in this book are those of Standards Australia. All cup and spoon measurements are level:

- The Australian Standard measuring cup has a capacity of 250 millilitres (250 ml).
- The Australian Standard tablespoon has a capacity of 20 millilitres (20 ml).

In all recipes metric equivalents of imperial measures are shown in parentheses e.g. 1 lb (500 g) beef. For successful cooking use either metric or imperial weights and measures—do not mix the two.

Weights

Imperial	Metric
$1/3$ oz	10 g
$1/2$ oz	15 g
$3/4$ oz	20 g
1 oz	30 g
2 oz	60 g
3 oz	90 g
4 oz ($1/4$ lb)	125 g
5 oz ($1/3$ lb)	150 g
6 oz	180 g
7 oz	220 g
8 oz ($1/2$ lb)	250 g
9 oz	280 g
10 oz	300 g
11 oz	330 g
12 oz ($3/4$ lb)	375 g
16 oz (1 lb)	500 g
2 lb	1 kg
3 lb	1.5 kg
4 lb	2 kg

Volume

Imperial	Metric	Cup
1 fl oz	30 ml	
2 fl oz	60 ml	$1/4$
3 fl oz	90 ml	$1/3$
4 fl oz	125 ml	$1/2$
5 fl oz	150 ml	$2/3$
6 fl oz	180 ml	$3/4$
8 fl oz	250 ml	1
10 fl oz	300 ml	$1 1/4$
12 fl oz	375 ml	$1 1/2$
13 fl oz	400 ml	$1 2/3$
14 fl oz	440 ml	$1 3/4$
16 fl oz	500 ml	2
24 fl oz	750 ml	3
32 fl oz	1 L	4

Oven temperature guide

The Celsius (°C) and Fahrenheit (°F) temperatures in this chart apply to most electric ovens. Decrease by 25°F or 10°C for a gas oven or refer to the manufacturer's temperature guide. For temperatures below 325°F (160°C), do not decrease the given temperature.

Oven description	°C	°F	Gas Mark
Cool	110	225	$1/4$
	130	250	$1/2$
Very slow	140	275	1
	150	300	2
Slow	170	325	3
Moderate	180	350	4
	190	375	5
Moderately Hot	200	400	6
Fairly Hot	220	425	7
Hot	230	450	8
Very Hot	240	475	9
Extremely Hot	250	500	10

Useful conversions

$1/4$ teaspoon	1.25 ml
$1/2$ teaspoon	2.5 ml
1 teaspoon	5 ml
1 Australian tablespoon	20 ml (4 teaspoons)
1 UK/US tablespoon	15 ml (3 teaspoons)

Butter/Shortening

1 tablespoon	$1/2$ oz	15 g
$1 1/2$ tablespoons	$3/4$ oz	20 g
2 tablespoons	1 oz	30 g
3 tablespoons	$1 1/2$ oz	45 g